# RESTAURANT
# COOKBOOK

# RESTAURANT
# COOKBOOK

By John Uglesich

Photography by Neil Alexander

**PELICAN PUBLISHING COMPANY**
Gretna 2004

*The word "Pelican" and the depiction of a pelican are trademarks
of Pelican Publishing Company, Inc., and are registered
in the U.S. Patent and Trademark Office.*

**Library of Congress Cataloging-in-Publication Data**

Uglesich, John.
    Uglesich's Restaurant cookbook / John Uglesich.
        p. cm.
    Includes index.
    ISBN 1-58980-209-8 (hardcover : alk. paper)
    1. Cookery (Seafood) 2. Cookery—Louisiana—New Orleans. 3. Uglesich's
Restaurant—History.  I. Title.

    TX747.U34 2004
    641.6'92—dc22

                                          2004008090

Printed in Singapore
Published by Pelican Publishing Company, Inc.
1000 Burmaster Street, Gretna, Louisiana 70053

# Contents

*Dedicated
in loving memory to
Tweety Uglesich
Thank you for twenty-two years of happiness.*

*And to
Edward F. Flettrich
I love you, Daddy.
The world does not seem right without you.*

*And to
Sam M. Uglesich
My best friend*

*Anthony and Gail Uglesich*

# An Open Letter

This cookbook has been created through over seventy years of hard work and an appreciation of each and every customer that has every patronized Uglesich's restaurant. We have always prided ourselves in serving each and every customer with a quality product. The following pages will provide a history of the restaurant, its owners, special customers, vendors, and of course recipes. We hope you enjoy the cookbook, as much as, we have enjoyed your support.

Anthony Uglesich                                    Gail Uglesich

*The staff of Uglesich's*

# Acknowledgments

A huge thanks to my parents, Anthony and Gail. Without their years in hard work of making Uglesich's a national success, I would not have had the opportunity to write this cookbook. You both have been the best parents, in providing me with an education and supporting me in making my own decisions. Your belief in my ability to write and organize this cookbook was extraordinary. I hope I have made you both proud of me.

Donna, you are my sister and one of my best friends. You looked out for me when we were children and still do today. You have my complete trust. I enjoy your company and I know I can always depend on you. Thanks for being my personal editor.

A special thanks to my grandfather Sam Uglesich. Without his hard work and foresight Uglesich's would not exist today. To my grandmother Emily Uglesich for all of the compliments and encouragement you have given me through the years.

To my grandparents Ed and Jo Flettrich. You are my extra set of parents. Thank you both for helping to raise me, and always taking me on your vacations. You taught me how to invest in the stock market, had the belief in me to manage the company portfolios, and always provided me with resources for a better life. I appreciate everything you have given me. It has made me a better person.

Katie, with those big brown eyes, you are not treated as a dog, nor do you act like one. Your bark is worse than your bite.

Nina Kooij, Dr. Milburn Calhoun, James Calhoun, Terry Callaway, and the entire staff of Pelican Publishing: you have made me feel like a part of the family. I look forward to working with you again in the future.

To my aunts, uncles, and cousins: I thank you for your help with the history of the restaurant and for your continued love and support.

David, Nissa, Stroddle, Peanut, and Chan: you are with me *four* life. I am proud to introduce you among my best friends. Through good or bad times, I know you are only a phone call away. I am blessed to have you both in my life. Thank you for everything.

Pam and Dr. Volek, thanks for your funny stories and jokes. As much as I love to laugh, I am the worst at repeating any of your jokes.

Frank Triche, thanks for helping me so much with my computer. It was near death several times, but you were able to resuscitate it each time.

A huge thanks to National Fence Corporation for the use of the office and all the equipment.

To the booster club members and its presidents, thank you for being so nice and welcoming me into the TU family.

Mr. Paul, you introduced me to new people and put in the good word to get me into the Field of Dreams.

Coach Abadie, Ronnie, Dr. Watts, Sal, Bill, Phil, Don, Paul, and Nick: you are all truly the Field of Dreams. I appreciate how you have accepted me into your group and look forward to playing baseball every Saturday morning.

Thanks to Jose and Katie for the lessons and your friendship.

Thanks to all of my friends at the bank and their former employees.

Thanks to Alba, Todd, Tina, Don, Linda, Lou, Gretchen, Monte, Patty, David, Nissa, and Donna: you truly are my brothers and sisters.

Elvis, sing me some songs.

And finally, to photographer Neil Alexander: thank you for all of your photographs, including the cover shot, all the food plate items, and my personal portrait. Your work and dedication are extraordinary. I hope to work with you again.

# Introduction

Both local and out of town visitors have had an attraction to this small neighborhood restaurant. Uglesich's (pronounced U-GUL-SICH's) seafood restaurant is a family-owned business that has never expanded and has been in the same location since the 1920s. Sam Uglesich started the restaurant and today it is owned and operated by Sam's son Anthony and his wife, Gail. Tony and Miss Gail, as the customers like to call them, have taken a restaurant once known only for fried seafood plates or sandwiches to a restaurant offering appetizers and specialty dishes that have been featured on *Emeril Lagasse's Super Bowl Bash* special and *Martha Stewart Weekday Living* shows. The restaurant has never advertised, and has prospered because of numerous articles that have appeared in newspapers and magazines that have propelled customers to try this New Orleans tradition.

Located on the corner of Baronne and Erato, the old tan wood building trimmed in light blue is surrounded by brick sidewalks. A large Uglesich's sign hangs above the canopy surrounded by an image of a shrimp, crab, oyster, and fish. The original double, wood French doors provide entrance at the front and side of the building, while the name Uglesich's is painted on the three glass windows. Next to the restaurant is the free, open gravel parking lot providing ample space.

The restaurant is open for lunch only Monday through Friday, as well as the two Saturdays during Jazz Fest, which is the last weekend in April and the first weekend in May. The doors open at 10:30 A.M. and with a first-come-first-served policy, a line usually develops fast outside the door. No reservations are accepted, and the small restaurant has only ten tables inside. Eight years ago six tables were added outside along the building. Customers arrive by car or taxi, or have walked the two blocks from the streetcar line on St. Charles Avenue. It is not uncommon for customers to arrive directly from the airport—or before their departing flight—with their luggage still in their possession, to eat at the restaurant.

When entering the building, a two-sided laminated menu is provided, and customers approach Anthony and Gail, who are located behind the long, stainless steel counter with marble top, to place their order. Anthony, a stout man with very short gray hair and glasses, feels most comfortable wearing his traditional T-shirt and Bermuda shorts, while Gail is often compared to Nancy Reagan, because of her slender build and short red hair. Behind Anthony and Gail is another counter displaying all the drinks available for purchase. Those include red and white wine, a service provided following the request of customers about ten years ago, both imported and exported beers, only Coca-Cola soft-drink products, tea, and water.

Once the order is received, it is brought to the kitchen, and each customer receives a number written on a small yellow paper, while waiting for the next available table. Cash or travel-check payments only are accepted before proceeding to the end of the counter or oyster bar. At the bar, Michael Rogers is shucking oysters and placing them on the half shell. The wall behind Mr. Rogers proudly displays his first-place plaque for being the fastest oyster opener in the city. Customers can view the open kitchen while Anthony Rogers is washing all silverware and plates, Zena Cooper is frying or sautéing the seafood items in the old black pots and pans, Cynthia Mack is preparing all main entries, and Michelle Rogers is preparing the appetizers.

When your number is called, one of the tables with wooden chairs is now available. Shortly, John Rea will serve your appetizers first, and later the main entries will arrive with fresh French bread. Coffee was served but discontinued sometime in the late 1950s. Dessert has never been offered.

New Orleans is one of the top tourist destinations in the world, so it is no wonder today that 80 percent of the restaurant's clientele consist of tourists. This unique cookbook contains old, current, and new recipes that have been and will be offered in the restaurant, as well as a complete history of the restaurant, from its founder, Sam Uglesich, to the current owners, Anthony and Gail Uglesich. Readers will discover interesting stories about George Fisher, the "Singing Bread Man," Ding Ding, the "King of the Hawkers," who made deliveries for the restaurant, and the very first private party thrown by Ahmet and Mica Ertegun, then head of Atlantic Records, for Sid Bass and his wife. The experience of Uglesich's restaurant as well as the awesome food have made this small family restaurant a New Orleans tradition since 1924.

# RESTAURANT
# COOKBOOK

Chapter One

# The Owners

*Sam Uglesich*

# Sam Uglesich

## The Founder

Sam Maté Uglesich founded Uglesich's Restaurant in 1924. Sam was born in the village of Bozava in Dugi Otak, Yugoslavia, a very poor country with many of its people starving. Hoping to start a better life, he unsuccessfully tried to come to America in 1918. But at the age of twenty he was successful in his second attempt, arriving by boat in 1920. He left behind his three brothers and three sisters to start a new life, and ultimately a better life for his future family.

Upon his arrival in the United States, he did not speak English, but found work in the restaurant business, which was owned by Yugoslavians. For the next four years, Sam learned and spoke the English language with a heavy accent. He saved enough money to open his own seafood and po-boy restaurant on South Rampart Street. In 1927, he obtained a lease agreement and moved the restaurant to its current location between Baronne and Erato streets.

It was at the restaurant that he met one of his neighbors, Emily Grandeury Perry, and her two children, Ruth and Gloria. Due to his accent, he called her "Emme," and the couple dated for about one year and were married in 1937. Emily and Sam had two children, the first a boy named Anthony, and the second a girl named Carol.

Sam was good hearted, and it was not uncommon for him to treat some customers to their food, if they were starving or short on cash. He would send packages of clothing, as well as money, to his family in Yugoslavia. From 1927 until the 1950s, the restaurant was open from 9 A.M. to 2 A.M. every day of the week, serving breakfast, lunch,

*Sam and Emily Uglesich*

and dinner. Sam sponsored his brother, Tony, who came to America to help manage the family restaurant.

The menu was limited and consisted of egg, ham, roast beef, fried oyster and shrimp po-boys, as well as oysters on the half shell. The only plate items offered were fried oyster, shrimp, trout, or a combination. The restaurant consisted of only the two brothers, Helen, a long-time employee, and an oyster opener. They all worked extremely hard, with customers shouting their orders from front to back. Today, Anthony and Gail marvel at how they were able to keep everything straight.

Sam's only break came every Thursday night when the family gathered to have dinner or to attend a movie. His favorite food was garlic, and would routinely eat it with just bread. Today, a dish is proudly named in his behalf, Sam's Favorite, because it is prepared with lots of garlic.

As the brothers grew older, they decided to reduce the number of hours the restaurant was open. Tony passed away in 1964, a couple of months after his retirement. In 1969, Sam was diagnosed with prostate cancer, which led to his passing in 1974. Sam was able to visit his homeland several times, and was extremely proud that he was alive to see his son Anthony and his wife, Gail, take over the family business.

# Anthony Uglesich

## Co-Owner

Since he was a teenager, Anthony has worked in the restaurant, learning the trade from his father, Sam, and Uncle Tony. He opened oysters, cleaned fish and shrimp, waited on the tables, and worked in the kitchen. Upon graduating from Fortier High School, Anthony attended Louisiana State University for a half semester. He left school to work full-time in the restaurant upon the passing of his Uncle Tony. Anthony later was drafted to serve his country during the Cuban Missile Crisis. After his two-year stint in the army, he returned to work full time in the restaurant, learning to manage the family business.

A typical day for Anthony begins at home on the telephone ordering produce and bread and checking on the delivery time with his usual suppliers. By 8:30 A.M., Anthony has arrived at the restaurant with his car full of plastic containers and pots that hold some of the sauces, gumbo, soups, and casseroles that were prepared the night before and in the morning. Before the restaurant opens, Anthony is busy making his own sauces and preparing such items as Mama's pasta, stuffed crabs and stuffed bell peppers. He also accepts and checks on all deliveries, and helps the employees with their prep work.

Anthony is known for having a good sense of humor and an open personality. He will help guide each customer to the popular dishes, new items, or the fresh seafood that arrived and is honest when a particular seafood is not offering the quality, size, or taste that is expected upon dining at Uglesich's. Anthony proudly states, "People trust me. If something's not running good, I'll say 'look, don't get it.'"

For instance, usually in the month of September oysters are small and not recommended. The untrue myth is that oysters run well in months that end with the letter "R." If a customer routinely orders the same item, it is not uncommon for Anthony to try to persuade that customer to try something new or different. He likes to give the example of a customer who had been coming in for years and had always ordered the shrimp po-boy. Anthony talked him into trying Paul's Fantasy, and to this day, the customer will not order anything else.

Upon the last customer's departure, Anthony is busy cleaning and washing the restaurant for the next business day. In his forty-five years of working at Uglesich's, Anthony has missed only two working days. Both times it was because he had undergone orthoscopic knee surgery.

Like his father, Sam, Anthony has always been proud that Uglesich's serves only fresh Louisiana seafood and not the less inexpensive imported food. Longstanding relationships have been developed with Louisiana suppliers for purchasing shrimp from Bobby Schwab, catfish and alligator from Joey and Jeannie Fonseca, and oysters from P & J Oysters. Anthony's integrity for the product being served is well respected by his peers and clientele.

# Gail Uglesich

## Co-Owner

Gail is the second of two daughters of Ed and Jo Flettrich. Upon graduating from Ursuline High School, she attended three and half years of college at Loyola University, before transferring to the University of New Orleans. After a serious car accident, she was forced to drop out of college, but later received an internship as a student teacher in Jefferson Parish. She became a full-time teacher, instructing fourth and fifth grades, and would later meet Anthony on a blind date.

After her marriage, Gail left teaching and became involved in the restaurant by doing prep work in the kitchen. She did not know how to cook, yet self-taught herself to prepare meals for both herself and her husband. With her family expanding, Gail decided to work at home by rearing her children, yet still prepared dishes for the restaurant. It was during this time that she started to experiment with different dishes, and like today, Anthony was her tester.

With the children grown, Gail returned to the restaurant working twice a week, and continued to prepare dishes from home. As the business continued to grow, so did her work schedule. Today, she wakes up at 4:30 in the morning to begin preparing from scratch all the sauces, crab cakes, casseroles, gumbo, and other specialty dishes. Working every day, she arrives at the restaurant around 11 A.M. greeting customers as they walk through the door. She takes the customers' orders, makes all mixed drinks, and when needed cleans the tables and helps in the kitchen.

After she departs the restaurant at 4 P.M., Gail arrives at home to take care of the house and prepares dinner for her family. Like Anthony, her routine is the same the very next business day.

*Anthony and Gail Uglesich*

# Anthony and Gail

## Working as a Team

Anthony and Gail met on a blind date that was set up by a mutual friend. They dated for approximately one year and were married on December 28, 1963. After their marriage, the couple decided to take a loan and purchase the land and building where Uglesich's currently resides, and in 1966 purchased the restaurant from Sam Uglesich.

In 1974, Anthony and Gail began to expand the menu that today includes appetizers, soups, salads, and specialty items that are now barbecued, grilled, marinated, or sautéed, while still preserving the traditional fried seafood plates and sandwiches. Anthony and Gail work as a team, investigating and testing all new recipes by viewing cooking shows, reading numerous cookbooks and the food section of several national newspapers, and dining at restaurants across the United States. By substituting ingredients or adding to the seasoning to help bring out the taste, their version of the new recipe begins to take shape. It is then tested and tasted several times, before the final product is available. Both Anthony and Gail readily admit they are not chefs, yet classify themselves as cooks.

Owning and managing the restaurant requires Anthony and Gail to work seven days a week, while their weekends are occupied purchasing products and preparing the appetizers and sauces. As noted by Chef Emeril Lagasse, "Their teamwork is about 75 percent of their success." Both are committed to one another and to the restaurant. When asked why customers keep returning to Uglesich's, Gail quickly credits Anthony's personality and honesty in providing customers with a good quality product. While Anthony believes customers "come for my wife Gail's food. Our fish is fresh every day, straight from the waters. We buy most of our seafood directly from the fisherman and shrimpers—no middleman holds it up and adds his tariff, which is why our prices are fair." It is this through this teamwork that Uglesich's is still a New Orleans tradition.

# A Daughter and a Son

## Donna Uglesich and John Uglesich

Anthony and Gail have two children, a daughter, Donna, and a son, John. Like most parents, they wanted to give their children a chance for a quality education and an opportunity to have a better life. They worked extremely hard to finance their education and are proud that both children received a college degree.

Having graduated from McGehee School in 1982, Donna attended and graduated from Tulane University with a bachelor of arts degree in Sociology. She later received her master's from Tulane University in social psychology. Today she is the manager and president of National Fence Corporation, which was started by her grandfather. John graduated from De La Salle High School in 1986 and graduated from Tulane University with a bachelor of arts degree. He actively manages stock portfolios.

Many people have questioned whether Donna or John will take over the family business. Both have seen first hand how their parents have dedicated their lives seven days a week while continuing to manage and oversee every aspect of the business. Neither Anthony nor Gail forced their children into the business and they respect them for having made their own career decisions.

Chapter Two

# Former Greats

Since 1924, many dishes have been served at Uglesich's. These included: Fried Egg Sandwich, Fried Chicken, Spaghetti and Meatballs, Smothered Cabbage, Marinated String Bean Salad, and Red Beans and Rice. These great recipes and many others were replaced when the restaurant began to barbecue, grill, marinate, or sauté only seafood items.

# ABBREVIATIONS
## Standard

tsp.   =   teaspoon
tbsp.  =   tablespoon
oz.    =   ounce
qt.    =   quart
lb.    =   pound

## Metric

ml.    =   milliliter
l.     =   liter
g.     =   gram
kg.    =   kilogram
mg.    =   milligram

## STANDARD-METRIC APPROXIMATIONS

$\frac{1}{8}$ teaspoon   =   .6 milliliter
$\frac{1}{4}$ teaspoon   =   1.2 milliliters
$\frac{1}{2}$ teaspoon   =   2.5 milliliters
1 teaspoon     =   5 milliliters
1 tablespoon   =   15 milliliters
4 tablespoons  =   $\frac{1}{4}$ cup   =   60 milliliters
8 tablespoons  =   $\frac{1}{2}$ cup   =   118 milliliters
16 tablespoons =   1 cup    =   236 milliliters
2 cups         =   473 milliliters
$2\frac{1}{2}$ cups   =   563 milliliters
4 cups         =   946 milliliters
1 quart        =   4 cups   =   .94 liter

## SOLID MEASUREMENTS

$\frac{1}{2}$ ounce   =   15 grams
1 ounce    =   25 grams
4 ounces   =   110 grams
16 ounces  =   1 pound   =   454 grams

# RECIPES THAT HAVE APPEARED IN THE RESTAURANT

## Fried Egg Sandwich
### On French Bread

This sandwich was the only breakfast item offered in the restaurant and cost only fifteen cents. For an extra ten cents a cup of coffee could be purchased. The coffee was also brewed for Brown's Dairy, located across the street from the restaurant, to help produce their coffee ice cream. In the early 1970s, the item was discontinued when the restaurant cut back it long hours of operation. Anthony said this breakfast was *ummm ummm* good!

Butter or margarine
1 egg
Salt
Pepper
French bread
Mayonnaise

Melt butter or margarine in frying pan.

Break egg into pan.

Sprinkle with salt and pepper.

Break the yellow of the egg, so that it runs while cooking.

Turn egg over one time.

Toast French bread, spread the mayonnaise on the topside of the bread, and place the fried egg on the bottom side of the bread.

# Deep-Fried Chicken

## Notes

*If you would like more seasoning, then sprinkle hot sauce on top of fried chicken.*

*Thicker pieces take longer to cook, approximately 15 to 20 minutes.*

Fried chicken was served for many years, but was eliminated with the introduction of appetizers and sautéed dishes in the restaurant.

Chicken
2 cups of plain white flour
2 tsp. of salt
½ tsp. of black pepper
¼ tsp. of cayenne
1 tsp. of garlic powder
Canola oil

Cut up the chicken, then wash and pat dry with paper towel.

Add salt, black pepper, cayenne, and garlic powder to flour and mix.

Pour the canola oil into a fryer and heat to 350 to 375 degrees.

When oil is hot, lightly coat chicken with the flour mixture.

Place into fryer and turn each chicken over once.

Cook chicken until it turns golden brown. Test by sticking a fork in the chicken. If juice runs clear, the chicken is done.

*Window at Uglesich's advertising fried chicken*

# Chicken Gumbo

## Over Rice

Chicken gumbo is one Anthony's favorites and is sometimes prepared for customers upon request. It is prepared every year for our Thanksgiving dinner. This recipe will take two days to prepare.

## Day One

2 (3½ to 4 lb.) chickens, cleaned and washed
1 large onion, cut into six pieces
2 large carrots, each peeled and cut into four
    pieces
4 stalks of celery, each cut into four pieces
1 tsp. of salt
½ tsp. of black peppercorns

In a large pot place the chickens, onions, carrots, celery, salt, and black peppercorns.

Cover the chickens with cold water.

Bring to boil, then lower heat and cover pot, with a crack in the pot so that the water does not overflow.

Cook for approximately 1½ to 2 hours.

Turn off the fire and let cook.

When cool enough to handle, take the chickens out of the pot.

Remove the skin, and shred the meat off the bones.

Place the meat in a container and refrigerate until the next day.

Strain the broth, and when cool place in the refrigerator overnight.

# Day Two

¼ cup of canola oil
½ cup of flour
2 lb. of okra, washed and cut into
   ½-inch rounds
1 medium onion, chopped
2 stalks of celery, chopped
½ green bell pepper, chopped
1 bunch of scallions, chopped
   (white part only)
4 cloves of garlic, chopped
2 tbsp. of parsley, chopped
1 fresh bay leaf
½ to ¾ tsp. of dry thyme
½ tsp. of dry marjoram
½ tsp. of dry basil
1 can (28 oz.) of crushed tomatoes
1 lb. of ham, diced
2 lb. of country sausage, cooked and sliced
   into ¼-inch pieces
1 tsp. of Worcestershire Sauce
Salt
Black pepper
Cayenne
Hot sauce

Take out the cooked chicken meat and broth from the refrigerator.

Skim off the fat from the broth.

In a large pot, add the oil and set on medium heat.

When the oil is hot add the flour and make a roux (the color of peanut butter), which takes approximately 20 to 30 minutes.

Add the okra, onions, celery, bell peppers, scallions, garlic and parsley.

Cook until okra is no longer stringy; this should take approximately 1 hour.

Add bay leaf, thyme, marjoram, basil, crushed tomatoes, ham, and chicken meat from day one, and cooked sausage.

Cook all together for approximately 5 minutes.

Pour the broth, which is a thickened gel, into the pot.

Add the Worcestershire sauce.

Cover the pot and cook on a low fire for approximately $1\frac{1}{2}$ hours, stirring often.

Season with salt, black pepper, cayenne, and hot sauce.

Serve over cook rice.

# Spaghetti and Meatballs

In our home, spaghetti and meatballs is a traditional Thursday night dinner.

## Meatball

1 lb. of lean ground meat
½ lb. of lean ground pork
½ cup of plain breadcrumb
½ cup of imported grated Romano cheese
1 tbsp. of parsley, chopped
2 raw eggs
½ cup of Egg Beater
1 tsp. of salt
¼ tsp. of black pepper
Canola oil

In a large bowl, mix all ingredients, except canola oil.

Shape into a ball; size depends on individual.

Pour enough canola oil to coat bottom of frying pan, and set on medium heat.

Place the individual meatballs in pan, and fry until meatballs are brown on all sides.

Drain on a paper towel.

## Gravy

2 tbsp. of canola oil
1 medium onion, chopped
4 cloves of garlic, chopped
1 can (12 oz.) of tomato paste
2 cans (8 oz.) of tomato sauce

4 tbsp. of imported Pecorino Romano cheese
2 tbsp. of basil
Sugar, salt, and black pepper (optional)
Water

In a large deep pot, add the canola oil and set on medium heat.

Sauté the onions and garlic until translucent.

Lower the heat; add 1 can of tomato paste, constantly stirring so that the paste does not stick (cooking the paste down), for approximately 30 to 45 minutes.

Add tomato sauce and continue to stir for approximately 30 to 45 minutes, trying to get rid of the water released by the tomatoes.

Take pot off of stove, and take the empty tomato paste can and fill it up with water three times, and pour into pot.

Take empty tomato sauce can, fill each can with water three times, and pour into pot.

Add cheese and basil.

Add salt, black pepper, and sugar (only if desired).

Place back on stove on high heat until it comes to boil.

Cover the pot, lower heat to medium low, and cook for 1 hour.

Add the meatballs and cook until gravy turns thick, approximately 2 hours.

### Spaghetti

Cook as per directions on box.

When cooked, always rinse over cold water. This helps to prevent the pasta from sticking.

Add some of the cooked gravy to pasta.

Place back on stove and set on low heat to warm pasta for a couple of minutes.

Place the spaghetti on the plate, topped with the gravy and meatballs.

# Baked Macaroni
## With Three Cheeses

1 lb. of penne macaroni
1 can of evaporated milk
½ cup of Egg Beater
1 stick of margarine, cut into pieces
½ cup of shredded American cheese
½ cup of shredded mozzarella cheese
½ cup of shredded cheddar cheese
1 slice each of American, mozzarella, and
  cheddar cheese

Bake in a preheated, 350-degree oven.

Cook the penne macaroni according to package directions.

Drain into colander and rinse with cold water.

Grease a casserole dish; add the macaroni, milk, Egg Beater, margarine, and the cups of shredded cheeses.

Stir and place in oven.

Bake for approximately 30 minutes; take out of oven and stir.

Place bake in oven and bake for approximately 30 minutes.

Take out of oven, if cheese is all melted and the mixture is solidified, then add the individual slices of cheese on top.

Place back in oven, when the cheese melts it turns brownish and the casserole is complete.

# Black-Eyed Peas

## Note

*The black-eyed peas freeze well.*

Black-eyed peas are prepared for the holidays, and when eaten are supposed to bring good luck.

1 lb. of black-eyed peas
1 medium onion, coarsely chopped
1 small bell pepper, coarsely chopped
4 cloves of garlic, coarsely chopped
4 tender stalks of celery, coarsely chopped
½ lb. of chopped ham
½ to 1 tsp. of fresh thyme
2 qt. of water
1 can (8 oz.) of tomato sauce
2 tsp. of salt (optional)
½ tsp. of black pepper (optional)
¼ tsp. of cayenne (optional)

Rinse the black-eyed peas in colander.

Place in a large stockpot.

Add the onions, bell pepper, garlic, celery, ham, thyme, water, and tomato sauce.

If seasoning, add the salt, black pepper, and cayenne.

Stir and bring to boil.

Cover the pot and lower heat.

Cook for approximately 2 hours, constantly taking off the cover and stirring.

Cook until tender.

Water may be added if contents become too thick.

# Mardi Gras Salad

## With String Beans and Peas

1 can (14.5 oz.) of French-style string beans
1 can (15 oz.) of small, young tender peas
1 jar (2 oz.) of diced palmetto
1 small green bell pepper, chopped
1 small white onion, chopped
4 stalks of celery, chopped
½ cup of vegetable oil
⅔ cup of white wine vinegar
Salt
Black pepper

In a bowl, mix all the ingredients together, adding salt and pepper to taste.

Refrigerate before serving.

Placed desired portion over chopped lettuce.

### Note

*Please use the lettuce of your choice.*

# Smothered Cabbage

## Notes

*Cabbage throws off a lot of water, but sometimes water is needed to cook the cabbage down.*

*This dish is special because after its sits a day or two the flavors intensify.*

1 head of cabbage, coarsely chopped
1 tbsp. of canola oil
4 to 6 boneless top-loin pork chop
1 medium onion, chopped
2 to 3 cloves of garlic, chopped
1 apple, peeled, seeded, and cut into chunks
Salt, black pepper, and cayenne

Wash the cabbage in water and drain in a colander.

Pour the canola oil in a dutch oven pot and set on medium heat.

Season the pork loin with salt and black pepper.

Place in the pot and brown on brown sides.

Remove the meat and place on plate.

Add the onions and garlic to dutch oven pot and cook until translucent.

Add the drained cabbage and scrape the bottom of the pot for any brown bits that may have accumulated.

Season with salt, black pepper, and cayenne to taste.

Add the cut apple and pork loin.

Cover the pot and lower the fire. Cook until tender, stirring from the bottom to the top every 15 minutes. The cabbage will become brown.

# Smothered Pork Chops
## With Red Gravy over Egg Noodles

1 tbsp. of canola oil
6 half-inch-thick center-cut pork chops
Salt
Black pepper
2 cloves of garlic, finely chopped
1 medium white onion, finely chopped
2 cans (8 oz.) of tomato sauce
Water
1 bag of eggless egg noodles

Pour the canola oil in a skillet and set on medium heat.

Take the pork chops and season with salt and black pepper.

Place pork chops in skillet and brown on both sides.

Remove the pork chops, place the garlic and onions in skillet, and sauté until translucent.

Stir and scrap the bottom of the skillet for any brown bits that have accumulated.

Add the tomato sauce, and cook on low fire for approximately 20 minutes while occasionally stirring.

Fill the two tomato cans with water and pour into the skillet.

Add salt and black pepper to your taste, bring to boil, and then lower fire.

Place the pork chops in the skillet and cover.

Cook until pork chops turn tender for approximately 20 minutes.

Cook the egg noodles according to package directions.

Place pork chops with red gravy over egg noodles.

# Marinated String Bean Salad
## Over Lettuce

## Notes

*This recipe is best using fresh beans, due to drizzling the olive oil over the hot cooked beans. Canned beans can be used, but fresh beans are preferred.*

*To test if beans are cooked, take one bean and cut with spoon. If the bean cuts easily then it is cooked.*

*Always taste before moving to the next step.*

This recipe was developed and served for a friend of Ms. Lorraine Neville, who visited every year during Jazz Fest and has now passed away.

Prepare this recipe one day before serving.

1 lb. of fresh string beans
Extra virgin olive oil
Garlic, finely chopped
Parsley, finely chopped
Salt and pepper (optional)

Snap off end of string beans, break beans in half, wash, and then place in pot.

Cover with cold water and bring to a boil.

Add a teaspoon of salt.

Cover pot, lower to medium heat, and cook until beans are tender, approximately 30 to 45 minutes.

Strain beans in colander, place in bowl, and drizzle with extra virgin olive oil.

Add chopped garlic and parsley.

Season with salt and pepper to your taste.

Let cool and refrigerate overnight so beans can marinate.

Place beans over chopped lettuce.

# Cornish Hen

## Topped with a Glaze

The glaze recipe was given by a customer who suggested it be used on seafood. Anthony and Gail found that the glaze worked better on top of the Cornish hen.

## Glaze

2 tbsp. of Dijon mustard
2 tbsp. of pineapple preserve
2 tbsp. of apple jelly

Mix all ingredients together in a measuring cup.

2 Cornish hens
¼ stick of butter or margarine, melted
Salt and black pepper
Paprika

Preheat oven to 350 degrees.

Clean and wash the Cornish hen, cutting off all excess fat, and pat dry.

Place the Cornish hen in baking pan, breast side up, and pour butter or margarine over the hens.

Season with salt and black pepper both inside and outside of the hen.

Sprinkle paprika on top of hen.

Place in the oven and bake for 45 minutes.

Turn over the hens, adding some water and scraping the bottom of the pan.

Bake for another 45 minutes.

Pull out of oven and turn over the hens again, with the breast side being up.

Pour glaze over cooked hens.

Lower oven to 300 degrees and cook for 30 minutes.

More water may be needed, to make a sauce.

# Red Beans

## Served Over White Rice

This New Orleans tradition was served at the restaurant every Monday for twenty years.

1 package (1 lb.) of red beans
1 onion, chopped
1 bell pepper, chopped
2 stalks of celery, chopped
4 cloves of garlic, chopped
1 lb. of ham, chopped
2 ham hocks
1 can (8 oz.) of tomato sauce
2 tsp. of salt
$\frac{1}{2}$ tsp. of black pepper
$\frac{1}{4}$ tsp. of cayenne
1 stick of margarine or butter

Place red beans in pot and soak the beans in cold water over night.

Next morning rinse off the red beans, and place beans back in pot.

Again add water to one inch above the beans.

Add the onions, bell pepper, celery, garlic, ham, ham hocks, tomato sauce, salt, black pepper, and cayenne.

Bring to a boil, then lower fire and cover pot.

Cook until tender, which will take 2 to 3 hours.

Check on beans every 30 minutes by stirring and smashing beans against the pot; this helps prevent the beans from sticking.

After beans are cooked, add a stick of margarine or butter to make them creamy.

Serve beans over cooked white rice.

## Notes

*The beans freeze well.*

*To make beans soupier, add more water.*

# Club Sandwich
## Roast Beef, Bacon, and Swiss Cheese

This sandwich, one of Sam's favorites, was made on white toast and served many years ago.

6 slices of smoked bacon
3 slices of white bread
Several slices of roast beef
Mayonnaise
2 to 3 slices of imported Swiss cheese, thinly sliced
Lettuce
Tomato

Cook bacon until crisp, and drain on paper towel.

Toast the white bread.

On the first slice of bread stack the roast beef.

On the second slice of bread spread the mayonnaise.

Place second slice of bread on top of first slice of bread with roast beef.

On the third slice of bread add bacon, Swiss cheese, lettuce, and tomato.

Place the third slice of bread underneath the roast beef.

## Note

*Wheat bread can be substituted in place of white bread. Today, Anthony prefers the wheat bread.*

# Marinated Crab Fingers

This recipe is prepared when jumbo crab fingers are in season. It is a favorite of both Anthony and his daughter, Donna, who like to dip the French bread in the marinade to suck up the juices.

1 lb. of crab fingers
1 bunch of scallions, coarsely chopped
1 tbsp. of parsley, finely chopped
1 clove of garlic, pressed
Juice of 1 lemon
1 tsp. of salt
¼ tsp. of black pepper
½ cup of extra virgin olive oil
¼ cup of rice wine vinegar

Drain crab fingers in a colander and remove any loose shells.

Place the crab fingers in a container.

Add the scallions, parsley, garlic, lemon juice, salt, and pepper, and stir.

Pour in the olive oil and vinegar and mix well.

Cover the container and refrigerate for 1 to 2 hours to blend in the flavors.

## Note

*The longer the marinade sits, the better the taste.*

# Mirliton and Shrimp Casserole

## Notes

*Another name for mirliton is chayote.*

*Try to purchase a whitish-colored or pale mirlitons, instead of green, due to the fact they cook quicker.*

*Never overcook mirlitons because they will throw off a lot of water.*

The recipe was given to Gail by a family friend and is made especially for her daughter, Donna, for Thanksgiving.

4 large mirlitons or 6 medium mirlitons
1 stick of butter or margarine
1 bunch of scallions, chopped
1 medium onion, chopped
2 tbsp. of parsley, finely chopped
1 lb. of peeled shrimp, cleaned and deveined
$\frac{1}{2}$ to 2 cups of seasoned breadcrumb
Olive oil
Salt and black pepper, optional

Place the mirlitons in a large pot and cover with cold water.

Bring to a boil, cover the pot, lower the heat, and cook until tender. Test if tender by sticking a fork in mirlitons. They should take approximately 25 to 45 minutes to cook.

Drain and let cool.

When cool, cut the mirlitons in half, remove the seed, and peel the skin.

Cut the flesh into chunks and let drain in a colander because mirlitons hold a lot of water.

Place the butter in a large skillet and set on medium heat.

Sauté scallions, onions, and parsley until translucent.

Add the shrimp and cook until pink.

Add the drained mirliton chunks, and mix all together.

Fold the breadcrumbs into the mixture a little at a time. The goal is for the mixture to be firm and not soupy.

Season if desired.

Take the mixture and place into a greased casserole dish. Drizzle olive oil on top and bake at 350 degrees for 30 minutes or until golden brown on top.

# Crawfish Hugo

## Served over Cooked White Rice

3 sticks of butter or margarine
½ cup of onions, chopped
½ cup of green bell pepper, chopped
¼ cup of grated carrots
1 lb. of Louisiana crawfish tails
2 scallions, chopped
3 tbsp. of parsley, chopped
1 tbsp. of fresh basil, chopped
1 tsp. of salt
¼ tsp. of black pepper
⅛ tsp. of cayenne

Melt the butter or margarine in a frying pan.

Add the onions and bell pepper to the pan and sauté until translucent.

Add the grated carrots and crawfish tails and sauté for 10 minutes.

Add the scallions, parsley, basil, salt, black pepper, and cayenne.

Cook for 5 minutes.

Serve over cooked white rice.

# Catfish Dip

## Notes

*Smaller or younger catfish taste better.*

*Never overcrowd the pot.*

Joey and Jeannie Fonseca, who supply catfish and alligator meat to the restaurant, provided this recipe.

## Dip

1 (8 oz.) package of cream cheese
Juice of 1 lemon
10 green onions, minced (tops and bottoms)
Dash or two of hot sauce
½ tsp. of Worcestershire Sauce
1 tsp. of salt
¼ tsp. of black pepper
¼ tsp. of garlic powder
½ qt. mayonnaise

Mix all ingredients together and refrigerate overnight.

## Frying catfish

Canola oil
1 lb. of catfish filet
Egg Beater
Fine plain bread crumbs

Heat canola oil into frying pot at 350 to 360 degrees.

Cut catfish filets diagonally into one-inch pieces.

Dip catfish into Egg Beater, and then cover lightly with breadcrumbs.

Place into pot, and fry until golden brown.

Drain onto paper towels.

*Jeannie Fonseca holding catfish*

# Baked Shrimp
## With Garlic

¼ cup of butter or margarine, melted
¼ cup of olive oil
2 tbsp. of fresh squeezed lemon juice
1 tbsp. of Worcestershire Sauce
1 lb. of medium shrimp; peeled, tails left on,
   and deveined
1 tsp. of salt (optional)
¼ tsp. of black pepper (optional)
8 cloves of garlic, chopped
4 tbsp. of parsley, chopped
Imported Parmesan cheese
Paprika

Preheat oven to 350 degrees.

Place the butter or margarine, olive oil, lemon juice, and Worcestershire Sauce in a pot and cook on low fire for 10 minutes.

Place the shrimp in a baking dish and pour the sauce over the shrimp.

Add the salt and black pepper.

Spread the garlic over the shrimp, and then sprinkle with parsley, Parmesan, and paprika.

Bake in oven for 15 minutes.

## Notes

*Salt and black pepper are optional for this recipe.*

*¼ cup of butter equals a half stick of butter or margarine.*

# Crawfish Stew
## Served over Rice

5 tbsp. of canola oil
¼ cup of all-purpose flour
1 large onion, chopped
1 small bell pepper, chopped
1 bunch of scallions, chopped
1 stick of celery, chopped
1 can (10 oz.) tomatoes with chilies
1 can (8 oz.) of tomato sauce
1 lb. of crawfish tails
1 tsp. of salt
¼ tsp. of black pepper
⅛ tsp. of cayenne (optional)
1 tbsp. of Worcestershire sauce

Pour the canola oil in a dutch oven pot and set on medium heat.

When hot, add the flour and constantly stir for approximately 20 to 30 minutes until the roux turns dark brown.

Add the onions, bell peppers, scallions, and celery and sauté for approximately 5 minutes.

Add the tomatoes with chilies, tomato sauce, crawfish tails, salt, black pepper, cayenne, and Worcestershire Sauce.

Lower heat, cover pot, and cook for approximately 20 minutes.

Shut off the fire, stir, and let the stew sit so that all the flavors blend.

Prepare your desired rice and place the crawfish stew on top.

## Note

*If the sauce is too thick add a little water.*

# Smothered Shrimp

## Served over White Rice

Because of Anthony's snoring too loudly at night, Gail thought of smothering Anthony, but instead came up with a recipe entitled Smothered Shrimp.

1 stick of butter or margarine
1 small onion, chopped
1 green bell pepper, chopped
1 stem of celery, chopped
1 lb. of shrimp, peeled and deveined
2 cans (14.4 oz.) of stewed tomatoes
2 jalapeno peppers; remove seeds and chop
1 tbsp. of lemon juice
1 bunch of scallions, chopped
1 tbsp. of parsley, chopped
2 tbsp. of medium dry sherry
1 tsp. of salt
$\frac{1}{4}$ tsp. of black pepper
$\frac{1}{2}$ tsp. of cayenne

Melt the butter or margarine in a large skillet and set on medium fire.

Sauté the onions, bell peppers, and celery until translucent.

Stirring constantly, add the shrimp and sauté for approximately 5 minutes or until shrimp turn pink.

Add the stewed tomatoes and jalapenos and cook for another 10 minutes.

Add the lemon juice, scallions, parsley, sherry, salt, black pepper, and cayenne.

Cover and simmer for approximately 20 minutes.

Serve over cooked white rice.

# Smothered Potatoes

Canola oil
1 potato, peeled and vertically sliced into
 ¼ to ½ rounds
1 medium onion, vertically sliced into
 thin rounds
2 eggs, beaten
2 tsp. of parsley, chopped
Salt and pepper to taste


Spray the skillet with a non-stick spray.

Pour the canola oil into the skillet and set on medium heat.

When the skillet is hot, add the potato slices and brown on both sides.

Remove the potatoes from the skillet and add the sliced onions.

Saute the onions until translucent.

Return the potatoes to the skillet and add the eggs.

Add the parsley, salt, and pepper and prepare until eggs are cooked.

# Chapter Three

# Current Recipes

# Shrimp and Grits

## In Cream Sauce

The grits and sauce need to be prepared in advance in order to complete this dish.

1 box of grits
2 tbsp. of seafood seasoning
2 tbsp. of Worcestershire Sauce
White pepper
1 qt. of heavy cream
Medium shrimp, peeled and deveined
Canola oil
Egg Beater
Fine plain breadcrumbs

Prepare grits as per directions on box.

Pour cooked grits on a cookie sheet and set to harden.

Cut into triangles.

## Preparing the sauce

In a mixing bowl, add the seafood seasoning, Worcestershire Sauce, and white pepper. Mix well.

Slowly add the cream, and mix well.

Pour the sauce into a container and refrigerate.

When ready to use, shake up sauce and place the desired amount in a skillet and set on a medium fire.

## Notes

*The restaurant uses Cajun Land seasoning.*

*The restaurant uses three shrimp per grit triangle.*

When sauce comes to boil, add the shrimp, and cook until shrimp turn pink.

Pour the oil in deep fryer and heat oil to 350 to 360 degrees.

Pour the Egg Beater in a separate bowl and dip the grit triangles, then lightly coat with fine plain breadcrumbs.

Place coated triangles in fryer and cook until golden brown.

Let the fried grits drain on a paper towel.

Place fried grits on a plate and cover with the sauce and shrimp.

*Shrimp and Grits*

# Shrimp Cake Patties
## Topped with Chipotle Mayonnaise Sauce

2 lb. of cooked shrimp, cut up with scissors
4 tsp. of fresh tarragon, chopped
4 tsp. of fresh basil, chopped
4 tsp. of parsley, chopped
2 tbsp. of fresh chives, chopped
2 bunches of scallions, chopped
2 heaping tbsp. of mustard
2 tbsp. of mayonnaise
2 to 3 cups of plain breadcrumbs
1 to 1½ cups of Egg Beater
Butter or margarine

Pour all ingredients in a bowl, and mix together and form into a patty.

Place each patty on a tray, cover with plastic wrap, and freeze overnight.

Thaw the desired number of patties, pour butter or margarine into skillet, and set on a medium heat.

Place patties in skillet and sauté the shrimp cake on each side for 2 minutes.

Place patties on a plate and pour the chipotle sauce over each shrimp cake.

# Chipotle Mayonnaise Sauce
## Over Shrimp Cake

2 yellow bell peppers
4 cloves of garlic
2 chipotle peppers from the chipotle
   peppers in adobe sauce can
2 egg yokes
2 tsp. of salt
½ tsp. of black pepper
¼ tsp. of cayenne
1 cup of olive oil

Take the yellow peppers and cut in half and remove all seeds.

Roast the yellow peppers in a broiler until charred.

Place in a bowl and cover with plastic wrap and let them sweat.

When cool, peel the peppers and place them and the remaining ingredients in a blender.

While pureeing, slowly add the olive oil.

# Marinated Shrimp

Topped with Shallots, Celery, and
Parsley over French Bread

## Note

*Marinade will
preserve well in
the refrigerator for
several days; please
stir before using
again and settle at
room temperature.*

The marinade must be prepared first.

## Marinade

¼ cup of red wine vinegar
½ cup of olive oil
Juice of 1 lemon
2 cloves of garlic, pressed
1 tsp. of salt
¼ tsp. of black pepper

Pour vinegar into a container, slowly stream olive oil, and whisk into vinegar.

Mix the remaining ingredients together into a container.

French bread
Boiled shrimp
Celery, finely chopped
Shallots, finely chopped
Black olives, finely chopped
Parsley, finely chopped
Imported Reggiano grated Parmesan cheese

Slice French bread into three ½-inch rounds and toast.

Dip toasted French bread in the marinade and place on plate.

Peel and devein the boiled shrimp and dip in the marinade.

Place on toasted French bread.

Top with a little chopped celery, shallots, black olives, and parsley.

Sprinkle with imported Parmesan cheese.

# Shrimp and Sausage Patty
## Topped with Creole Mustard Sauce

## Note

*When shaping patties, use your hands, ice cream scoop, or measuring cup of your choice to make patties bigger or smaller.*

2 lb. of loose country sausage
1 lb. cooked medium shrimp, cut into thirds
1 medium onion, finely chopped
1 small bell pepper, finely chopped
2 cloves of garlic, finely chopped
2 tbsp. of parsley, finely chopped
¼ cup of milk
1 cup of breadcrumb
1 cup of imported Romano cheese
1 tsp. of salt
¼ tsp. of black pepper
2 jumbo raw eggs
½ cup of Egg Beater
Canola oil

Spray skillet with non-stick product, and cook sausage until it turns brown.

Drain sausage on paper towel.

Place sausage in large bowl.

Add shrimp, onion, bell pepper, garlic, and parsley.

Pour milk into bowl.

Add the breadcrumb and cheese.

Add salt, black pepper, eggs, and Egg Beater.

Mix well and shape into patties.

Place on tray and cover with plastic wrap and freeze overnight.

Pour canola oil in skillet, set on medium heat and take out desired number of patties.

When hot, place patties in skillet and cook for 2 minutes on each side.

Place patty on plate, and top with Creole Mustard Sauce.

# Creole Mustard Sauce

¾ cup of heavy cream
¼ cup of Creole mustard
¼ cup of sour cream
2 jalapenos, seeded and finely chopped
½ tbsp. of Worcestershire Sauce
Several dashes of Crystal Hot Sauce
Salt and pepper to taste

Place cream in saucepot, and boil over medium heat and reduce by one-third.

Add Creole mustard and sour cream.

Stir and cook for 1 to 2 minutes.

Add jalapenos, Worcestershire, Crystal Hot Sauce, salt, and pepper.

Mix all together and let cool.

Pour into bottle and refrigerate.

## Note

*Before using, let the sauce sit at room temperature.*

# Firecracker Shrimp

## With Special Barbecue and Horseradish Sauce

### Note

*Use only the amount needed. The sauce can be stored in an air-tight container in the refrigerator.*

This recipe was inspired by Patrick Clark's barbecue sauce found in his cookbook *Cooking with Patrick Clark.* Upon reading his cookbook, Gail wanted to add more spice, and thus Firecracker Shrimp was developed.

## Barbecue Sauce

1 large onion, chopped
2 cups of orange juice
1½ sticks of unsalted butter
1 qt. of ketchup
½ cup of lime juice
½ cup of apple cider vinegar
½ cup of dark brown sugar
1 tbsp. of salt
1 tbsp. of black pepper
2 tbsp. of dry mustard
2 tbsp. of hot paprika
1 tbsp. of crushed red pepper
1 heaping tsp. of cayenne
1 tsp. of garlic powder
1 tsp. of chili powder
2 tbsp. of hot sauce
2 tbsp. of tamarind paste
2 tbsp. of honey

Place onions in food processor with the motor running, then add ½ cup of orange juice.

In a large pot, melt butter on medium heat and add the onion puree.

Add the 1½ cups of orange juice, and the rest of the ingredients.

Stir and cook on low fire for approximately 25 minutes.

# Firecracker Shrimp

5 large shrimp
½ cup of barbecue sauce

Leave head and tail on shrimp, and peel the body off.

Place barbecue sauce in skillet and set on medium heat.

Place shrimp in skillet and cook until they turn pink (approximately 2 minutes on one side, and 1½ minutes on the other) side.

Remove shrimp from skillet and place on plate, pouring any extra sauce from the skillet on top of the shrimp.

# Horseradish Sauce

¼ cup of pure horseradish
¼ cup Creole mustard
1 cup of heavy whipping cream
1 tsp. of salt
¼ tsp. of black pepper
⅛ tsp. of cayenne

Mix all ingredients together in a bowl.

Drizzle a small amount on top of the shrimp.

### Note

*A 16 to 20-count shrimp with the heads on are best for this recipe.*

### Note

*Store the extra in an airtight container in the refrigerator. It will last for the duration of the code date on the whipping cream.*

# Crawfish Maque Choux

### Smothered with White Corn, Tomato, and Seasonings

## Notes

*Can or frozen corn can be substituted for fresh corn.*

*If using frozen crawfish tails, please rinse.*

1 cup of canola corn oil
1 bell pepper, finely chopped
1 large onion, finely chopped
2 to 4 stalks of celery, finely chopped
2 cans (4 oz.) of mushroom stem pieces
1 can (14.5 oz.) of diced tomatoes
2 cups of fresh white corn, cut from the cob
2 lb. of crawfish tails
2½ tsp. of salt
¾ tsp. of black pepper
¼ tsp. of cayenne
1 bunch of scallions, finely chopped
2 tbsp. of parsley, finely chopped
2 sticks of margarine or butter

In a large pot, pour the corn oil, and set on medium heat.

Add the bell pepper, onion, and celery and sauté until translucent for approximately 15 minutes, uncovered.

Add mushrooms, tomatoes, and corn into pot and cook until corn is tender.

Add crawfish tails, salt, black pepper, and cayenne into pot and cook for another 5 minutes, stirring in the scallions and parsley.

Add margarine or butter, cover the pot and cook until melted, and stir.

# Crawfish Balls

## With Asian Dipping Sauce

1 cup of onions, finely chopped
1 cup of bell peppers, finely chopped
1 cup of celery, finely chopped
2 lb. of peeled crawfish tails
2 cups of seasoned breadcrumbs
2 tsp. of Creole mustard
2 tsp. of fresh squeezed lemon juice
1 tsp. of hot sauce
2 jumbo raw eggs
½ cup of Egg Beater
2 tsp. of salt
½ tsp. of black pepper
¼ tsp. of cayenne

Mix all ingredients together in a bowl.

Take a melon scooper and shape into balls.

Place the balls on a non-stick cookie tray and freeze overnight.

Canola oil
Egg Beater
Fine breadcrumbs

Preheat canola oil in frying pot at 350 to 360 degrees.

Take frozen crawfish balls, dip into Egg Beater, and then lightly cover with breadcrumbs.

Place in pot and fry until golden brown.

Drain on paper towel.

# Vietnamese Dipping Sauce

## Notes

*Crushed red pepper can be substituted for the Thai Bird Chile.*

*This sauce will last for a couple of weeks when refrigerated.*

*This sauce can be used with any seafood.*

This sauce is used over the crawfish balls.

6 Thai Bird Chile, seeded and finely chopped
2 to 3 cloves of garlic, crushed in garlic press
6 tbsp. of sugar
3 tbsp. of fresh lime juice
2 cups of warm water
9 tbsp. of Nuoc Mam Fish Sauce
½ small carrot, shredded

Mix the chile, garlic, sugar, and lime juice in a mortar. Press with the pestle until it forms into a paste.

Place paste into a bowl.

Add the water, fish sauce, and carrots.

Stir and refrigerate for several hours.

# Stuffed Pasta Shell
Pasta Shell Stuffed with Shrimp and Crab Meat

1 ½ lb. pasta shells
1 lb. of claw crab meat
1 lb. of cooked shrimp, cut up
4 roman tomatoes, diced
1 cup of shredded Swiss cheese
1 cup of shredded mild cheddar cheese
1 bunch of scallions, chopped
1 tsp. of dry basil
2 tsp. of salt
½ tsp. of black pepper
¼ tsp. of cayenne
2 raw eggs
Egg Beater
Plain fine bread crumb
Canola corn oil

Cook the pasta shells as per directions on box.

In a large mixing bowl, combine the crab meat, cut-up shrimp, diced tomatoes, Swiss cheese, cheddar cheese, chopped scallions, dry basil, salt, black pepper, cayenne pepper, and two raw eggs.

Mix thoroughly with your hands.

Deposit one tablespoon of mixture into each cooked pasta shell.

Place the pasta shells onto a pan and cover with plastic wrap and place into the freezer overnight.

Upon taking the shells out of the freezer, pour the Egg Beater into one bowl, and pour the breadcrumb into a separate bowl.

Dip each frozen pasta shell into the Egg Beater and then onto the breadcrumb.

## Note
*Do not overload the fryer when frying.*

Pour the oil into a deep frying pot and set at 350 degrees.

To test if the oil is hot enough, throw a pinch of the breadcrumb into the oil; when it bubbles to the top, then it is ready to fry.

Place each pasta shell into fryer and turn over one time.

When they rise to the top and are golden brown, take out.

Let the fried pasta shells drain on a paper towel.

# Crab Meat au Gratin

## Casserole

A very good customer, Monroe Falterman, who asked Gail to prepare a good crab meat au gratin, inspired this recipe. Gail spent many hours researching and testing for this recipe, and it was Monroe's favorite dish. Monroe lost his battle to cancer several years ago, but is still the only customer to have eaten on three separate occasions at the restaurant in one day.

2 sticks of butter or margarine
Medium onion, finely chopped
1 cup of celery, finely chopped
½ cup of bell pepper, finely chopped
1 clove of garlic, finely chopped
2 tbsp. of parsley, finely chopped
2 bunches of scallions, finely chopped
½ to 1 cup of flower
2 cans of evaporated milk
6 egg yokes

½ cup of whipping cream
2 tsp. of salt
½ tsp. of black pepper
½ tsp. of cayenne
1 cup of shredded Swiss cheese
1 (4 oz.) jar of diced pimento, drained
2 lb. of jumbo lump crab meat
2 cups of shredded mild cheddar cheese

Preheat oven to 350 degrees.

Melt the butter or margarine in a large skillet and set on medium heat.

Add the onion, celery, bell pepper, garlic, parsley, and scallions. Cook until translucent.

Add flour and mix well.

Add evaporated milk and stir.

Add egg yokes, whipping cream, salt, black pepper, and cayenne and mix all together.

Cook on medium fire until it thickens.

Add Swiss cheese and pimento; when the cheese melts shut off fire and fold in the crabmeat.

Pour mixture into a greased casserole dish.

Add cheddar cheese on top and place casserole in oven.

Bake for 45 minutes to 1 hour, or until the cheese turns golden brown.

Cool down before serving.

# Fried Green Tomatoes

## Notes

*Never overload your fryer when frying.*

*Boiled shrimp or crabmeat can be placed on top of the fried green tomatoes before pouring the remoulade sauce.*

This appetizer was and still is the most popular item on the menu. After eating fried green tomatoes from Mrs. Joanne Clevenger's Upperline restaurant, Anthony and Gail created a new version with special flavors from the sauce.

Canola corn oil
Egg Beater
1 green tomato, sliced ¼-inch thick
Plain fine breadcrumbs

Pour the oil into a deep-frying pot and heat to 350 degrees.

Pour the Egg Beater into a bowl.

Dip the sliced green tomatoes into the Egg Beater and lightly coat with the breadcrumbs.

To test if the oil is hot enough, throw a pinch of the breadcrumb into the oil; if it bubbles to the top, then it is ready to fry.

Place the tomatoes into the fryer and cook on one side for 1 minute.

Flip the tomatoes to cook on the reverse side for 1 minute.

Take out tomatoes and drain on paper towel.

Top with a remoulade sauce.

*Fried Green Tomatoes*

# Oysters Shooters

## Sautéed in Olive Oil, Balsamic Vinegar, and Cane Syrup

## Notes

*The extra sauce can be refrigerated and used again.*

*One particular customer likes to use this sauce over his fried soft shell crab.*

Gail prepared this recipe on the "Martha Stewart Living" weekday show.

2 cups of olive oil
½ cup of balsamic vinegar
4 tbsp. of cane syrup
1 tsp. of salt
1 tsp. of black pepper
1 tsp. of cayenne
6 tsp. of sun-dried tomatoes
½ tsp. of dried oregano
½ tsp. of dried basil
½ tsp. thyme
6 raw oysters

Pour all the ingredients into a container, and stir well.

Pour the desired amount of sauce in a skillet, and set on medium heat.

Place oysters in skillet and cook until they curl.

Place the oysters either back on the half shell or in a ramekin dish.

Pour the extra sauce over the oysters.

# Stuffed Oysters

## Stuffing
1 cup of seasoned breadcrumbs
½ cup of imported Parmesan cheese
½ tsp. of salt
Juice of 1 large lemon
4 cloves of garlic, pressed
1 ½ tsp. of crushed red pepper
1 ½ tbsp. of parsley, finely chopped
¾ cup of olive oil

In a large bowl, mix the breadcrumbs, Parmesan cheese, salt, lemon juice, garlic, red pepper, and parsley all together.

Drizzle the olive oil and mix together.

## Oysters
3 raw oysters

Place oysters on a clean oyster shell if available.

Put a spoonful of dressing on top of each oyster, and place on pan.

Place pan under the broiler and cook until stuffing is toasted.

The oysters will shrink and the edges will curl up.

## Note
*The stuffing lasts well if placed in an airtight container and placed in the refrigerator.*

# Stuffed Artichoke Bottoms

## Notes

*Each stuffed bottom can be individually wrapped and frozen.*

*Claw or back fin crab meat are best used for this recipe.*

The artichoke bottoms make a great appetizer to serve at a party.

1 bunch of scallions, chopped
⅓ bunch of parsley, chopped
4 cloves of garlic, chopped
1 lb. of crabmeat
1 tsp. of salt
¼ tsp. of black pepper
⅛ tsp. of cayenne
6 tbsp. of imported Parmesan cheese
4 tbsp. of unseasoned breadcrumbs
6 tbsp. of extra virgin olive oil
4 can (13.75 oz.) of artichoke bottoms

Mix the above ingredients in a bowl, except for the artichoke bottoms.

Wash the artichoke bottoms, dry, and moisten each bottom with a little extra virgin olive oil.

Stuff each bottom with the mixing.

Heat in the microwave for approximately 20 to 30 seconds. If frozen, increase microwave time.

# Gator Stew

Joey and Jeannie Fonseca, who supply catfish, crab meat, and gator meat to the restaurant, provided this recipe.

2 lb. of gator meat
¼ cup of canola corn oil
1 large onion, chopped
½ cup of bell pepper, chopped
½ cup of celery, chopped
1 can (10 oz.) of diced Rotel Tomatoes with
  Green Chilies
1 jar (16 oz. to 20 oz.) of Ragu Traditional
  Spaghetti Sauce
2 small cans of Dawn Mushroom Steak Sauce
1 can (4 oz.) of diced mushrooms
1 bottle (2 oz.) of green pitted olives
1 jar (2.25 oz.) of sliced black olives
1 bottle of imported beer

Cut the gator meat across the grain into small pieces, place in a pot, and cover with water.

Place on stove and bring to a boil.

Cover the pot, lower the heat, and cook for half an hour.

Drain gator meat into a colander.

In another deep pot, add corn oil and set on medium heat.

Add the chopped onion, bell pepper, celery, tomatoes, Ragu sauce, mushrooms, olives, beer, and gator meat.

Mix well together, bring to a boil with the cover on the pot, and lower heat.

Cook for 2 hours and constantly stir to avoid sticking.

## Note

*A good quality beer is highly recommended. For this recipe the restaurant uses Perroni beer.*

# Vegetable Soup
## With Shrimp and Crab Meat

This recipe was inspired from reading *Savoy* magazine; Gail and Anthony later added shrimp and their blend of seasoning to give it a different flavor.

½ lb. of peeled baby carrots, chopped
1 medium Yukon Gold potato, peeled and
   cut into cubes
2 stalks of celery, chopped
1 medium yellow onion, chopped
½ box (10 oz.) of frozen corn kernels
1 box (10 oz.) of frozen string beans
½ box (10 oz.) of frozen lima beans
¼ box (10 oz.) of frozen peas
1 can (28 oz.) of crushed tomatoes
4 tbsp. of Worcestershire Sauce
2 tbsp. of Louisiana Crab Boil
1½ tbsp. of dry mustard
6 to 8 cups of water
1½ tsp. of salt
½ tsp. of black pepper
⅛ tsp. of crushed red pepper
1 lb. of medium shrimp, cleaned and deveined
1 lb. of claw crab meat, cleaned

In a large stockpot place the carrots, potatoes, celery, onion, all frozen vegetables, crushed tomatoes, Worcestershire Sauce, crab boil, dry mustard, water, salt, black pepper, and crushed red pepper.

## Notes

*Start off with 6 cups of water; if you desire to have the soup thinner, add more water.*

*Taste the soup; more seasoning may be needed.*

*The restaurant uses Cajun Land Seasoning.*

Bring to a boil, cover, and lower heat to a simmer.

Cook for approximately 1 hour or until vegetables are tender.

Uncover the pot and add the shrimp.

Cook until shrimp turn pink.

Fold in crab meat and cook for 30 minutes.

# Oyster Brie Soup

This soup is an ideal dish for those cool evenings.

**Note**

*Always view the code date on the whipping cream and Half and Half. The later the date on the whipping cream, the longer the soup will last in the refrigerator.*

1 qt. of freshly shucked oysters with liquid
½ stick of unsalted butter
2 bunches of scallions, finely chopped
5 stalks of celery, finely chopped
8 cloves of garlic, finely chopped
2 tbsp. of parsley, finely chopped
1 qt. of whipping cream
50 oz. of Brie cheese
1 pt. of Half and Half
2 tsp. of salt
½ tsp. of black pepper
¼ tsp. of cayenne
3 to 4 medium-cooked Yukon Gold potatoes, diced in 1-inch cubes

In a two-quart pot, poach the oysters in their own liquid.

Melt the butter in a large skillet on medium heat.

Sauté the scallions, celery, garlic, and parsley until translucent.

Add the whipping cream.

Peel the bloomy rind off of the Brie cheese, cut into small pieces, and add to the skillet.

Raise the fire to high to enable the cheese to melt.

Once cheese is melted, lower the fire to a simmer and add the poached oysters with liquid.

Add the Half and Half, salt, pepper, and cayenne and cook for 2 to 3 minutes.

Add the potatoes, stir, and turn off fire.

# Oyster Cocktail Sauce

¼ cup of ketchup
1 tbsp of extra virgin olive oil
1 slice of lemon juice
1 tsp. of hot horseradish
Couple of dashes of hot sauce
Couple of dashes of Worcestershire Sauce

Mix all ingredients together and place in a cocktail glass.

## Note

*The restaurant uses Lea and Perrins Worcestershire Sauce.*

# Horseradish Mayonnaise
## And Ketchup Sauce

## Note

*This sauce is great for dipping all the fried seafood, and for shrimp or lobster cocktails.*

1 cup of heavy mayonnaise
2 tbsp. of prepared extra heavy horseradish
Ketchup

Mix the mayonnaise and horseradish in a bowl.

Using a soufflé cup, pour half the horseradish mayonnaise sauce on one side, and then pour ketchup on the other side.

# Tartar Sauce

1 jar (16 oz.) of hamburger dill pickle slices
4 to 6 tbsp. of heavy mayonnaise

Drain the pickles in a colander.

Place the pickles in a food processor and pulse until coarsely chopped.

Drain the pickles in a fine towel, by squeezing out all the juice.

Add the pickles and mayonnaise to a bowl and stir.

## Note

*The tartar sauce can be refrigerated and will last until the code date on the mayonnaise jar.*

# Muddy Waters

## Note

*The dressing must be refrigerated, and can be used over salad or seafood.*

The restaurant uses this sauce over pan-fried trout or shrimp.

2 tbsp. of canola oil
2 tbsp. of flour
1 can (2 oz.) of flat anchovies, rinsed
8 cloves of garlic, sliced
2 jalapeno peppers, gutted and sliced
1 can (14 oz.) of fat-free chicken broth
Parmesan cheese

Pour the canola oil into a skillet and set on medium heat.

Add the flour and stir until a roux develops. The roux will turn a peanut butter color.

Place the anchovies into the skillet and smash into the roux.

Slowly stir in the chicken broth to form gravy.

Add the garlic and cook for approximately 5 minutes.

Add the jalapenos and cook for approximately 5 minutes.

Pour the sauce over the pan-fried trout or shrimp. Sprinkle with Parmesan cheese.

# Cleopatra Dressing

This dressing was named after Anthony and Gail's granddaughter, Katie, a King Charles Spaniel. Katie receives lots of love and is pampered enough to be given the nickname Cleopatra.

1 can (2 oz.) of flat anchovies
8 large cloves of garlic
4 tsp. of dry yellow mustard
½ cup of fresh lemon juice
½ tsp. of black pepper
4 jumbo raw eggs
2 cups of olive oil

Pour the anchovies, garlic, mustard, lemon juice, and black pepper into a food processor and blend.

With the motor still running, pour the eggs into the processor.

Slowly drizzle the olive oil and blend.

# Shrimp Uggie
## Spicy Dish Served with New Potatoes

This recipe was named after Anthony and Gail's son, John Uglesich. His favorite seafood is shrimp. He was given the nickname of "Uggie" while in grade school because his classmates found it difficult to pronounce his last name. This dish is marinated in vegetable oil, with crushed red pepper, hot sauce, onion, and bell pepper added, and then sautéed.

3 cups of vegetable oil
1 cup of ketchup
½ bottle (5 oz.) of Melinda extra hot sauce
2 tbsp. of fresh lemon juice
2 tbsp. of salt
2 tsp. of fresh parsley, finely chopped
2 tsp. of paprika
4 tsp. of crushed red pepper
1 small purple onion, coarsely chopped
1 green bell pepper, coarsely chopped
8 to 10 medium shrimp, peeled and deveined,
    with tails left on
2 small-to-medium red or Yukon Gold potatoes

Mix all the ingredients, except the shrimp and potatoes, together in a container and let marinate.

Refrigerate for one day.

Boil potatoes and cut into 1-inch cubes.

Place skillet on stove and set on medium heat.

Upon taking the sauce out of refrigerator, stir really well; using a ladle, pour from the bottom to the top of container the desired amount into a skillet. Pour enough marinade to partly cover the shrimp.

Place shrimp and potatoes in skillet.

Cook both the shrimp and potatoes, constantly stirring and turning until shrimp turn pink.

Pour shrimp, potatoes, and all the sauce onto a plate and sprinkle with parsley.

*Shrimp Uggie*

# Voodoo Shrimp

## Shrimp over Pasta

Angel hair pasta
1 tbsp. of olive oil
½ small onion, chopped
2 cloves of garlic, chopped
½ tsp. of black bean sauce
1 tsp. of sugar
1 bay leaf
Salt
Black pepper
8 large shrimp; peeled, deveined, tails left on
1 sprig of fresh rosemary
4 pitted black olives, sliced in half
1 Roma tomato, julienne

Cook the angel hair pasta as per directions on box.

Pour the olive oil into a skillet, and set on medium heat.

When hot, add the onions, garlic, black bean paste, sugar, and bay leaf.

Sauté until translucent.

Salt and pepper shrimp and add to the skillet.

Stir constantly until shrimp turn pink.

Add the rosemary, olives, and tomatoes and stir.

Place pasta on plate.

Remove bay leaf; pour shrimp and sauce over pasta.

Voodoo Shrimp

# Italian Trout, Catfish, or Shrimp

This recipe is Gail's favorite in the restaurant. It is light, healthy, and offers great flavors. The trout, catfish, or shrimp is dipped in olive oil, then in a breadcrumb and imported cheese mixture. Then it is sautéed and fresh lemon juice squeezed on top.

## Breadcrumb and imported cheese mixture

4 cups of unseasoned fine breadcrumbs
2 cups of imported Pecorino Romano cheese
2 tbsp. of granulated garlic
2 tsp. of salt
¼ tsp. of black pepper
½ cup of dry parsley flakes

Mix all the ingredients in a big bowl.

Take amount needed, store the rest in a Zip Lock bag, and place in the refrigerator.

## Sautéing seafood

1 to 2 tbsp. of regular olive oil
Shrimp, trout, or catfish
Extra virgin olive oil
Lemon, cut into 6 pieces

Pour olive oil in a skillet and set on medium heat.

Take the desired seafood and dip in extra virgin olive oil.

Lightly coat the seafood with the breadcrumb mixture.

Place seafood into heated skillet and cook for approximately 2 minutes on each side.

Remove seafood from skillet and squeeze fresh lemon juice on top.

*Italian Trout, with a side order of Jambalaya*

# Grilled Seasoning

Chef Paul Prudhomme inspired this seasoning. It is used over all grilled products before cooking at the restaurant.

24 tsp. of salt
10 tsp. of cayenne pepper
12, ½ tsp. of thyme
12, ½ tsp. of oregano
12 tbsp. of sweet paprika
12 tsp. of onion powder
12 tsp. of garlic powder
10, ¾ tsp. of black pepper
10, ¾ tsp. of white pepper

Pour all ingredients in an airtight jar and shake until well blended.

## Note

*The butter and seasoning form a sauce that can be used on top of this dish.*

# Paul's Fantasy

## Pan-fried Trout Topped with Grilled Shrimp and New Potatoes

This recipe was named after Paul Varisco, who has been patronizing Uglesich's for over thirty years. The restaurant was separately offering grilled shrimp and pan-fried trout as entrees. Paul suggested combining the two dishes into one entrée. Anthony and Gail named the dish in his honor, and it is one of the most popular items on the menu.

5 tbsp. of butter or margarine
Trout (1 to 2 medium filets) or catfish
   (4 to 5 small filets)
Egg Beater
Plain fine breadcrumbs
6 to 8 medium raw shrimp; deveined and
   butterflied
Shallots, chopped
Parsley, finely chopped
1 slice of lemon

Melt 3 tablespoons of butter or margarine in skillet and set over medium heat.

Dip catfish or trout filets in Egg Beater, then lightly bread fish with breadcrumbs.

In the heated skillet, cook the fish on each side for approximately 3 to 5 minutes.

In a separate skillet, melt 2 tablespoons of butter or margarine and set on medium heat.

Place shrimp in skillet and sprinkle the grilled seasoning on top.

Cook on one side and then turn shrimp over and sprinkle more grilled seasoning.

Cook until shrimp turn pink.

Place fish on plate and top with shrimp, sprinkle with shallots and parsley.

Place lemon on side of plate, then prepare Seasoned New Potatoes recipe and place on side of dish.

Paul's Fantasy, with a side order of cole slaw

# Seasoned New Potatoes

## Placed on the Side of Paul's Fantasy

## Notes

*Red or Yukon Gold potatoes can be used for this recipe.*

*The Seasoned New Potatoes could be used as a side item for any seafood plate.*

1 to 2 potatoes (depending on size)
1 tbsp. of butter or margarine

Wash the potatoes and boil in a pot of water, then cook until fork tender.

Set on medium heat and melt butter or margarine in skillet.

Cut the potatoes into 1-inch cubes and coat the potatoes with the butter or margarine.

Sprinkle the grilled seasoning on potatoes and cook for 1 to 2 minutes.

Place the new potatoes on the side of the fish and shrimp of Paul's Fantasy.

# Crab Meat and Potato Patties

## Exactly What It Sounds Like

Emily Uglesich used to make codfish balls, which was a New Orleans tradition on Fridays. Gail did not care for the smell of the codfish, so she decided to substitute crab meat for the codfish and produced this new version. Anthony loved the new recipe and wanted it served in the restaurant.

2 large Yukon gold potatoes
1 lb. of white crab meat
1 lb. of claw crab meat
1 large onion, finely chopped
2 bunches of scallions, finely chopped
¼ cup of parsley, finely chopped
2 tsp. of salt
½ tsp. of black pepper
¼ tsp. of cayenne
½ to 1 cup of Egg Beater
Butter, margarine, or canola oil

Boil the potatoes until fork tender.

When cool, peel the potatoes.

Clean the crab meat by removing all loose shells.

In a large bowl, break the potatoes by hand.

Add the onions, scallions, parsley, crab meat, salt, black pepper, and cayenne.

Add the Egg Beater and mix everything by hand.

Form into patties.

Place the butter, margarine, or canola oil into non-stick skillet and set on a low heat.

Cook on one side for 2 to 3 minutes, then turn and cook on the other side for 2 to 3 minutes.

Place on paper towel and pat dry.

## Notes

*The patties freeze well.*

*The potatoes will turn brown because the product is already cooked.*

*Barbecued Shrimp*

# Barbecued Shrimp

## And New Potatoes

This barbecue sauce is one of the versions used in this region. When Anthony and Gail's son, John, dines at the restaurant, he always orders this entrée.

5 cups of butter or margarine
2½ cups of olive oil
5 tsp. of lemon juice
5 tbsp. of fresh basil, finely chopped
5 tbsp. of Worcestershire Sauce
5 tbsp. of coarse black pepper
5 tsp. of salt
20 cloves of garlic, coarsely chopped
1 whole lemon, thinly sliced
6 shrimp; slit back of shrimp, leaving body
   in tact
2 small cooked Yukon potatoes cut into
   1-inch cubes

Mix all the ingredients, except the shrimp and potatoes, together in a container; stir well, place top on container, and refrigerate for one day.

When ready to use, stir well again.

Place skillet on stove and set on medium heat.

Using a ladle, pour the desired amount into the skillet, scooping from the bottom and pouring enough to partly cover the shrimp.

Place the shrimp and potatoes in the skillet, set on low-medium heat, and stir.

Constantly turning the shrimp, cook until they turn pink.

Place shrimp, potatoes, and sauce all from the skillet onto a plate.

## Notes

*The barbecue sauce refrigerates well.*

*Use French bread to soak the excess sauce and eat.*

*Oysters or soft shell crabs can also be used for this dish. Cook the oysters until they curl; the soft shell crab will change colors.*

# Mamma's Pasta

## Notes

*Depending on the number of people served, the leftovers can be refrigerated or frozen.*

*As the dish sits, the flavors intensify.*

This recipe was named after and inspired by Anthony's mother, Emily Uglesich. It contains olive oil, butter, tomatoes, artichoke hearts, and shrimp served over pasta.

5 sticks of butter or margarine
1 cup of olive oil
1 bunch of scallions, chopped
10 cloves of garlic, sliced
2 cans (14.5 oz.) of artichoke hearts
7 Roma tomatoes, julienne
1½ lb. of clean medium shrimp, peeled
   and deveined
1 tbsp. of fresh basil, chopped
1 tbsp. of fresh parsley, chopped
2 tsp. of salt
½ tsp. of black pepper
1 tsp. of cayenne

Melt the butter or margarine in a large pot on medium heat.

Pour in the olive oil.

Sauté the scallions and garlic until translucent.

Add the artichoke hearts, tomatoes, and shrimp.

Cook until shrimp turn pink.

Add basil, parsley, salt, black pepper, and cayenne and mix well.

Pull off the fire and let it sit to cool.

# Sam's Favorite

## Served with New Potatoes

This dish is named in honor of Anthony's father, Sam Uglesich, because it contains two of his favorite ingredients: olive oil and garlic. The trout or catfish is sautéed with garlic, olive oil, basil, and Worcestershire Sauce.

2 small Yukon Gold potatoes
Olive oil
2 or 3 shakes of Worcestershire Sauce
Trout or catfish, removing the bones and skin
Salt
Black pepper
Dry basil
4 cloves of garlic, thinly sliced

Clean potatoes, boil in water, and then cut into 1-inch cubes.

Pour olive oil in skillet and set on medium heat.

Shake Worcestershire Sauce on olive oil.

Season trout or catfish on both sides with salt, black pepper, and basil.

Place trout or catfish in the heated skillet.

Cook approximately 2 to 3 minutes, turn the fish, and add the garlic and potatoes to the skillet.

Cook the other side of the fish for approximately 1 minute.

Turn the potatoes to pick up the seasoning.

# Stuffed Shrimp
### Large Shrimp Stuffed with Crab Meat, and Deep-fried

## Stuffing recipe
¼ stick of butter or margarine
1 cup of onions, finely chopped
½ cup of celery, finely chopped
¼ cup of bell pepper, finely chopped
1 clove of garlic, finely chopped
1 bunch of scallions, finely chopped
1 tbsp. of parsley, finely chopped
1 lb. of white crab meat
1 tsp. of salt
¼ tsp. of black pepper
⅛ cayenne
2 raw eggs, beaten
¼ cup of white flour

In a large skillet, melt the butter or margarine and set on medium heat.

Add onions, celery, bell pepper, garlic, scallions, and parsley and sauté until translucent.

Clean the crab meat of any loose shells and add to the skillet.

Add the salt, black pepper, cayenne and stir.

Add the eggs, sprinkle the flour, and mix well.

Let the stuffing sit in the refrigerator for several hours before stuffing the shrimp.

# Shrimp recipe

2 lb. of jumbo shrimp; peeled and deveined
Egg Beater
Fine breadcrumbs

Take the shrimp and cut the back halfway down.

Flatten the shrimp with your hands and place stuffing in middle.

Fold the shrimp over, and spear the shrimp with a toothpick from the tail to the top of the shrimp.

Place on a pan cover with plastic wrap and freeze overnight.

Preheat the oven to 350 to 360 degrees.

Take the desired amount of stuffed shrimp.

Dip into Egg Beater and then lightly coat with fine breadcrumbs.

Place into fryer, and fry until golden brown.

When they turn golden brown, place on paper towel.

Pat dry and cool.

Pull the toothpick out and serve.

# Crawfish Etouffe
### Served over Cooked White Rice

## Notes

*This recipe freezes well.*

*If using frozen Louisiana peeled crawfish tails, please wash the fat off the crawfish before cooking.*

*If using fresh crawfish, the fat helps to enhance the flavor.*

This recipe was inspired by Leon E. Soniat Jr.'s cookbook *La Bouche Creole*.

1 stick of margarine or butter
3 cloves of garlic, medium chopped
1 green bell pepper, medium chopped
2 stalks of celery, medium chopped
1½ cups of white onion, medium chopped
¼ cup of tomato paste
2 tbsp. of all-purpose flour
1 lb. of Louisiana crawfish tails
½ tsp. of chili powder
1 tbsp. of fresh squeezed lemon juice
½ tsp. of dry basil
¼ tsp. of dry thyme
1 cup of water
1 tsp. of salt
¼ tsp. of black pepper
⅛ tsp. cayenne
3 scallions, medium chopped
¼ cup of parsley, finely chopped

In a large pot, melt the stick of margarine or butter on medium heat.

Place the garlic, bell pepper, celery, and onion in the large pot and sauté vegetables until translucent.

Place the tomato paste and all-purpose flour into the pot and mix together.

Combine the crawfish, chili powder, lemon juice, basil, and thyme in the pot.

Add the water and stir.

Cover the pot, lower the fire, and cook for approximately 15 minutes.

Add the salt, black pepper, cayenne, scallions, parsley, and stir well.

Cover the pot and cook for another 15 minutes.

Serve over cooked rice.

# Shrimp Creole

## Cooked with Every Tomato Product You Can Imagine

Notes

*The Shrimp Creole is served over rice at the restaurant.*

*This recipe freezes well.*

½ cup of vegetable or canola oil

¾ cup of all-purpose flour

½ cup of onions, coarsely chopped

½ cup of celery, coarsely chopped

¼ cup of bell peppers, coarsely chopped

½ cup of scallions, coarsely chopped

2 cloves of garlic, finely chopped

2 tbsp. of parsley, finely chopped

1 can (8 oz.) of tomato sauce

1 can (6 oz.) of tomato Paste

1 can (14.5 oz.) of diced tomatoes

2 tsp. of salt

½ tsp. of black pepper

¼ tsp. of cayenne

4 dashes of hot sauce

2 fresh bay leaves

1 tbsp. of lemon juice

1 to 2 cups of water

2 lb. of shrimp, peeled and deveined

2 tbsp. of medium dry sherry

In a dutch oven, heat the oil on medium heat.

When hot, add the flour to make a roux, constantly stirring so as not to burn the flour.

Continue to stir until the flour turns the color of peanut butter.

Lower heat.

Add onions, celery, bell peppers, scallions, garlic, and parsley and cook until translucent.

Add tomato sauce, tomato paste, and diced tomatoes and stir; cook for approximately 2 minutes.

Add the salt, black pepper, cayenne, hot sauce, bay leaves, and lemon juice and mix well.

Stir in 1 to 2 cups of water.

Raise the heat until pot comes to a boil.

Lower heat, cover pot, and let sauce cook for approximately 1 hour.

Constantly stir so that the sauce does not stick to the bottom of the pot.

Add the shrimp, cover the pot, and cook for approximately 15 minutes or until shrimp turn pink.

Add the sherry, stir, and shut off the fire.

# Crawfish Fettuccini

## Cooked in Half and Half with Cheese

1½ sticks of butter
1 cup of onions, finely chopped
½ cup of scallions, finely chopped
3 tbsp. of garlic, finely chopped
¼ cup of flour
½ qt. of Half and Half cream
¼ cup of parsley, finely chopped
1 lb. of crawfish tails
¼ cup of Reggiano Parmesan
¼ cup of Pecorino Romano Cheese
2 tsp. of salt
½ tsp. of black pepper
¼ tsp. of cayenne

Place the butter in the skillet and set on low heat.

When melted, add the onions and scallions and sauté until translucent.

Add the garlic, and cook for 1 or 2 minutes.

Blend the flour into the sauce.

Slowly add the cream, and mix well.

Then add the parsley and crawfish tails.

Raise to medium heat.

When the sauce comes to a boil, stir in the Parmesan and Romano cheese.

Add the salt, black pepper, and cayenne.

Lower heat and simmer for 5 minutes.

Place over the fettuccini.

# Plates

*Plate of raw oysters*

# Soft Shell Crab

Canola oil
Egg Beater
1 soft shell crab, cleaned
Plain fine breadcrumbs

Clean the soft shell crab by removing the eyes and the tip of the mouth.

Lift up the upper shell and remove the gills, the feather-like objects, on both sides. Feel for the bag or sack and remove on each side. Take the bottom of the crab and remove the "apron" (the triangle shape) of the crab. Wash the crab with cold water and pat dry.

Pour canola oil into a fryer and set at 375 degrees.

Pour the Egg Beater in a bowl, and dip the soft shell crab.

Lightly cover the soft shell crab with the breadcrumbs, as well as underneath the shell.

Place the soft shell crab into the fryer and fry until golden brown on one side.

Using tongs, fry the other side of soft shell crab until golden brown.

Take out of fryer, and drain on paper towel.

Season with salt and black pepper to your taste.

*Fried Soft Shell Crabs*

# Stuffed Bell Peppers
## With Crab Meat and Whole Shrimp

## Notes

*Individually wrap the bell pepper and freeze.*

*Upon reuse, simply place in microwave.*

*Use the crab meat of your choice.*

12 bell peppers
2 sticks of butter or margarine
1 large onion, chopped
4 to 5 stalks of celery, chopped
2 tbsp. of parsley, chopped
2½ lb. of raw shrimp
7-oz. bag of stale pistolettes, moistened in water
1 lb. of crab meat
3½ tsp. of salt
1 tsp. of black pepper
¾ tsp. of cayenne
Seasoned breadcrumbs

Remove the top and seeds of bell peppers, cut in half, and wash.

Bring a pot of water to a boil and place peppers in the water.

Bring water back to a boil and boil for only 2 minutes.

Remove peppers from water and let cool.

Place the butter or margarine in skillet and set on medium heat.

When hot, sauté the onion, celery, and parsley until translucent.

Add the whole shrimp, and cook until they turn pink (approximately 5 minutes).

Squeeze the water out of the pistolettes, break into small pieces, and add to the shrimp mixture.

Add the crab meat, salt, black pepper, and cayenne.

Remove from fire and let stuffing cool.

Stuff the peppers and sprinkle each pepper with seasoned breadcrumbs.

Preheat the oven to 350 degrees.

Cook the stuffed bell peppers for approximately 30 to 45 minutes; the seasoned breadcrumb will turn brown.

# Stuffed Crab
## With Crab Meat

2 cups of milk or water
7-oz. bag of stale pistolettes
3 sticks of butter or margarine
1 large red, yellow, and green bell pepper, chopped
½ cup of scallions, chopped
1 medium onion, chopped
¼ tsp. of thyme
2 to 3 cloves of garlic, chopped
1 to 2 bay leaves
2 stalks of celery, chopped
1 lb. of claw crab meat
2 lb. of white crab meat
3 tsp. of salt
¾ tsp. of black pepper
⅜ tsp. of cayenne

## Note

*The aluminum crab foil can be purchased in any grocery store.*

*Any extra crab meat mixture can be placed in individual Zip Lock bags and frozen.*

Pour the milk or water into a bowl and soak the pistolettes.

Squeeze the pistolettes and break into small pieces.

Melt 2 sticks of butter or margarine in frying pan on medium heat.

Saute the peppers, scallions, and onion for 5 minutes.

Add the thyme, garlic, and bay leaf and cook for 10 minutes.

If mixture is dry, add another stick of butter or margarine.

Add celery and saute for 5 minutes.

Add the squeezed pistolettes to the frying pan and mix well.

Add the claw and white crab meat, salt, black pepper, and cayenne and mix all together.

Preheat oven to 350 degrees.

Put crab meat mixture into a greased baking pan and cook for approximately 30 minutes. The top will turn brown.

Take out desired amount and place on individual aluminum crab foil.

# Crab Cake

## Topped with Corn Salsa

## Notes

*Lump crab meat is expensive.*

*White or claw meat can be combined and used for this recipe.*

*Use only the amount of crab patties desired; the others can be frozen.*

2 lb. of crab meat
2 bunches of scallions, chopped
2 tsp. of parsley, chopped
2 tbsp. of chives, chopped
2 tbsp. of mayonnaise
2 tbsp. of Creole mustard
2 cups of breadcrumbs
4 raw eggs
2 tsp. of salt
½ tsp. of black pepper
¼ tsp. of cayenne
Canola corn oil

In a large mixing bowl, add the crab meat, scallions, parsley, chives, mayonnaise, mustard, and breadcrumbs.

Crack the eggs and pour into the bowl.

Add the salt and black and cayenne pepper.

Mix well with your hands.

Shape into a patty and place on a tray. Cover with plastic wrap.

Place the tray into the freezer and keep overnight.

Add corn oil to the skillet and set on medium heat.

When hot, place the patty in the skillet and fry on each side for 2 minutes.

Remove from skillet and place the fried patty on a paper towel to drain.

Place the patty on a plate and top with the Corn Salsa.

# Corn Salsa
## Over Crab Cakes

4 Roma tomatoes, diced
1 can (11 oz.) of Summer Sweet Corn
2 seeded jalapeno, diced
1 small purple onion, diced
1 red, yellow, and green bell pepper, diced
1 bunch of cilantro, chopped
½ cup of olive oil
⅓ cup of red wine vinegar
2 tsp. of salt
½ tsp. of black pepper

Place all above items in a bowl and mix together.

Refrigerate until ready to use.

# Oyster or Shrimp Po-Boy

## Notes

*The number of oysters or shrimp to place on the loaf depends on the size.*

*Cream meal is the finer version of corn meal.*

Oyster po-boy was the first item offered in the restaurant. In the 1920s a sandwich cost only five cents while the loaf cost ten cents. The Oyster Po-Boy was prepared on television for the "Martha Stewart Living Weekday Show," as well as and Ti Martin's "My Country My Home" special. Both ladies marveled at the taste and believed it was the best oyster po-boy they have eaten.

Canola corn oil
Oysters or shrimp (medium)
Cream meal
French bread
Salt and pepper

Heat the canola corn oil to between 350 and 360 degrees. Throw a pinch of the cream meal into the oil; if it pops, the oil is ready to fry.

Lightly coat the oyster or shrimp with the cream meal. Add the oyster or shrimp one at time into fryer.

Do not overload fryer.

The oyster or shrimp will rise to the top when cooked. The shrimp will cook quickly. The cooking time for the oysters depends on the size.

Remove from fryer, drain on paper towel, and add salt and pepper.

Toast French bread.

Place oyster or shrimp on the bottom of the French bread. Use your choice of dressing on the top portion of French bread.

*Oyster Po-Boy*

# Super Slaw

## Notes
*Refrigerate the dressing.*

*The dressing will last until the code dates on the mayonnaise and sour cream.*

This recipe was inspired upon reading the food section of the local newspaper *The Times-Picayune*.

First prepare the dressing.

## Dressing
2 cups of mayonnaise
½ cup of sour cream
¾ cup of Creole mustard
2 tbsp. of lemon juice
4 tsp. of sugar substitute
2 tsp. of salt
½ tsp of black pepper

Mix all ingredients together in a bowl.

## Super Slaw
1 pkg. of mixed cole slaw
Handful of baby spinach, removing the stems
Red, yellow, and green bell peppers, sliced into strips
Pickle jalapeno, diced
Medium shrimp, cooked
Cole slaw dressing

Mix all ingredients together in a bowl, using the desired amount of cole slaw dressing.

# Dirty Rice
## Beef Sausage Cooked over White and Wild Rice

1 lb. of long grain white rice
¼ lb. of wild rice
1 lb. of beef sausage
Canola corn oil
1 onion, diced
4 cloves of garlic, finely chopped
1 bunch of scallions, diced
4 stalks of celery, diced
1 bell pepper, diced
2 tbsp. of parsley, finely chopped
1 can (4 oz.) of chopped mushrooms
1 jar (4 oz.) of diced pimento
3 tsp. of salt
½ tsp. of black pepper
¼ tsp. of cayenne

Cook the white and wild rice as per directions on box in separate pots.

Take the beef sausage and cut ¼-inch thick, then take the ¼-inch piece and cut into 4 separate pieces.

Spray the skillet with a non-stick product.

Place the sausage in the skillet and cook for 5 minutes on medium heat.

Drain the sausage on a paper towel.

In another skillet, pour 1 to 2 tablespoons of the canola oil and set on medium heat.

When hot, combine the onion, garlic, scallions, celery, bell pepper, and parsley and sauté until translucent.

Drain the mushrooms and pimento into a strainer, and place into the skillet.

Add the cooked beef sausage and mix together.

Place the mixture into a large bowl.

Add the cooked white and wild rice to the bowl.

Add the salt, black pepper, and cayenne, and mix well together.

Note

*Any leftovers can be placed in a freezer bag.*

# Potato Salad

## Notes

*The amount of mayonnaise needed depends on how creamy you want the potato salad.*

*Salt and pepper are not needed, but provide seasoning.*

There are many different versions of potato salad. This particular recipe has been used in the restaurant for thirty years and was provided by Anthony's mother, Emily Uglesich.

5 lb. bag of Yukon Gold potatoes
2 stalks of celery, chopped
1 bunch of scallions, chopped
1 small white onion, chopped
2 tbsp. of fresh parsley, finely chopped
3 jumbo hardball eggs
1 tsp. of yellow mustard
3 tsp. of salad vinegar
4 to 5 tsp. of regular olive oil
Mayonnaise

Boil the potatoes until tender, let cool, then peel the skin and slice the potatoes into $1/2$-inch cubes.

Place cubed potatoes in a large mixing bowl, and add the chopped celery, scallions, onions, and parsley.

Peel the hardball eggs, cut the eggs in half, and take out the yoke and place in separate bowl.

Dice up the white egg and place in a large mixing bowl.

Smash the yoke and combine the yellow mustard, vinegar, and olive oil.

Mix together and place the mixture into the large mixing bowl.

Add mayonnaise to mixing bowl.

Add salt and pepper for seasoning, if necessary.

Mix well together.

*Emily, Anthony, and Gail Uglesich*

# Onion Rings

## Fresh

### Note

*Place each onion ring separately in the fryer, and do not overload the fryer.*

1 onion
Canola oil
2 cups of flour
2 tsp. of salt
½ tsp. of black pepper
Egg Beater

Cut the onion rings to your desired thickness.

Pour the oil in the fryer and heat at 350 degrees.

Pour the flour in a large Zip Lock bag.

Add the salt and pepper to the Zip Lock bag and shake well.

Pour the Egg Beater in a bowl.

Dip the cut onions in the Egg Beater and put into the Zip Lock bag.

Shake off any excess flour from onion rings.

Place the onions in the fryer and cook until golden brown.

Drain onion rings on a paper towel.

Add salt and pepper on top if desired.

# French Fries

A customer from Belgium who told Anthony how to make the fries crispier inspired this recipe.

3 large Idaho potatoes
Water
Canola oil
Salt

Using a potato peeler, peel the skin from the body, but leave the skin on the top and bottom of the potato.

Cut into thick or thin slices.

Place the potatoes in a bowl and cover with cold water. This will remove the starch from the potatoes. This procedure may have to be done twice.

Pat the potatoes dry.

Pour the oil in the fryer and set at 350 degrees.

When oil is hot, parboil the potatoes for 1 minute.

Take out of the fryer and let the potatoes cool.

Raise the fire to 365 degrees and place fries back into the oil.

Cook until golden brown.

Place fries on paper towel and drain.

When hot, sprinkle the desired amount of salt.

## Note

*The thinner fries cook quicker and are crispier.*

# Jambalaya

## Note

*The jambalaya freezes well, but remove all bay leaves before freezing.*

This recipe was inspired while dining at Stephen Pyle's restaurant in Las Vegas. Gail and Anthony purchased his cookbook *New Tastes From Texas*. Gail later added her mixture of herbs and seasonings to the recipe.

¼ cup of olive oil
½ lb. of smoked andouille sausage, sliced and diced
¼ lb. of tasso, sliced and diced
2 cups of onions, finely chopped
1 red pepper, finely chopped
1 green bell pepper, finely chopped
4 to 6 stalks of celery, finely chopped
6 large cloves of garlic, finely chopped
1 bunch of scallions, finely chopped
3 cans (14.5 oz.) of diced tomatoes, drained
1 tbsp. of fresh oregano, finely chopped
2 tsp. of fresh basil, finely chopped
1 tbsp. of fresh cilantro, finely chopped
1 tsp. of fresh thyme, finely chopped
3 bay leaves
1 tsp. of ground cumin
3 tsp. of salt
½ tsp. of black pepper
¼ tsp. of cayenne
2 cans (14 oz.) of chicken broth
1 lb. bag of long-grain white rice
2 lb. of shrimp, peeled and deveined

Pour the olive oil into a deep large skillet.

Sauté the sausage and tasso on medium heat for approximately 5 to 10 minutes.

Add onions, red and green peppers, celery, garlic, and scallions and sauté until translucent.

Add the tomatoes, oregano, basil, cilantro, thyme, bay leaves, cumin, salt, pepper, and cayenne and stir.

Add the chicken broth, raise heat to high, and let it come to a boil.

After it comes to a boil, add the rice and stir.

Lower heat and cover the pot.

Cook until almost all the liquid is absorbed, for approximately 20 to 25 minutes.

Add the shrimp and place the cover back on the pot for approximately 15 minutes or until shrimp are pink.

Pull pot off the fire and let it sit for approximately 15 minutes, then stir again.

# Eggplant Casserole

## Note

*The casserole freezes well, but remove bay leaves before freezing.*

8 medium eggplants
2 sticks of butter or margarine
2 cups of onions, finely chopped
⅓ cup of bell pepper, finely chopped
3 to 4 large cloves of garlic, finely chopped
⅓ cup parsley, finely chopped
3 bay leaves
1 lb. of ham, finely diced
1½ lb. of shrimp, cooked
2 raw eggs, whipped
3 tsp. of salt
½ tsp. of black pepper
¼ tsp. of cayenne
1 tbsp. of fresh thyme, finely chopped
1 to 2 cups of plain breadcrumbs

Preheat oven to 350 degrees.

Place the eggplant in a large pot and cover with water.

Let the water come to a boil and cook until a fork can easily pierce the stem of the eggplant; depending on the size of the eggplant, cook for approximately 15 to 20 minutes.

Drain the eggplant and let cool before handling.

Peel the eggplant and slice and dice into small pieces into a colander. This helps the eggplant to drain because of the amount of water it retains.

In a large skillet, melt the butter or margarine and set on medium heat.

Sauté the onions, bell pepper, garlic, and parsley until translucent.

Add the bay leaves and ham and cook for approximately 5 minutes.

Add the drained eggplant and cook for approximately 5 minutes.

Place the eggplant mixture into a large mixing bowl.

Add the shrimp (if large, cut in half), salt, black pepper, cayenne, and thyme.

Add the egg and mix well.

Add the breadcrumbs to help stiffen the casserole and mix.

Pour this mixture into a large baking pan and bake in oven.

Cook for approximately 45 minutes.

Chapter Four

# Suppliers, Distinctive People, and Events of the Restaurant

*George "The Bread Man" and Anthony Uglesich*

# Leidenheimer Bakery

## The Singing Bread Man

Leidenheimer Bakery is the only bakery that has supplied French bread and breadcrumbs to the restaurant. George Leidenheimer, founder of the bakery in 1896, came to the United States from Deidesheim, Germany. All breads are made fresh in the bakery warehouse. They are available for shipment throughout the country and are delivered on a daily basis to local restaurants and stores.

George Fisher, a delivery man for Leidenheimer for thirty-six years, delivered bread to Uglesich's for twenty years. He was known as the Singing Bread Man, and by the end of the workday would return to the restaurant with his tape cassette and sing to the customers famous songs by his two favorite performers, Al Jolsen and Engelbert Humperdinck. George took very good care of all of his clients, and would routinely make two or three trips a day to check to see if more bread was needed.

Upon his retirement from the bakery, George could still be seen at the restaurant, cleaning the tables, greeting the customers, or singing his favorite songs. Today, George is officially retired, but still makes an occasional appearance at the restaurant.

# P & J Oysters

## Only the Best Will Be Accepted

P & J Oysters has supplied fresh oysters for many years to the restaurant. John Popich and his partner, Joseph Jurisich, whose family was in the oyster business, started the company in 1876. As success came, John and Joseph added a salesman, Alfred Subseri, who was married to Joe's first cousin. Alfred later became the third owner, and brought his son Sal to work in the business. Today, Sal's three children, Al, Sal, and Meri, run P & J Oysters.

The three owners understand Anthony is very particular and picky about his oysters. According to Meri, "He'll pay extra for the big shells, because he knows his clientele and that's how he likes to present them." Before any sacks are purchased, Anthony inquires about the size and flavor. Because oysters are extremely popular with the customers and are used for many dishes, Anthony will accept only the best.

*Bobby Schwab, the Shrimp Man*

# Bobby Schwab

## The Shrimp Man

Bobby Schwab, who was born and reared in New Orleans, started his career as an electrician, but because of a poor work economy needed to find another business. While most of his friends were moving to the East Coast for better job opportunities, Bobby decided to stay home and find employment to help support his mother. He purchased approximately 250 pounds of shrimp from a shrimp troller and approached several restaurants about purchasing his new product. After the 250 pounds were sold, he acquired more shrimp and ultimately his new career had begun.

George Fisher, the Singing Bread Man, first introduced Bobby to Anthony. Their relationship has prospered for twenty years, with the two men developing a mutual respect for each other because of their honesty in business. Bobby has repeatedly said that customers like Anthony are almost as extinct as a dinosaur, because he personally checks the quality of all deliveries. Uglesich's, is one of the fifteen restaurants that Bobby delivers shrimp to in the New Orleans area.

*Ding Ding, the King of the Hawkers*

# Ding Ding

## King of the Hawkers

Ambrose Schumpbert, most commonly known as Ding Ding, was an orphan reared by priests. He was extremely recognizable around New Orleans, due to his selling beer, peanuts, and popcorn at all sporting events at City Park and the old Pelican and Tulane stadiums. Anthony and Ding Ding first met at a playground when they were children and stayed friends until the latter's death.

From 1970 to 1982, the restaurant offered a delivery service in the downtown New Orleans Business District. For three hours a day, Ding Ding would ride a bicycle to make his deliveries. He was well liked by the customers and often was described as simple with a great personality.

After making deliveries, Ding Ding would return to the restaurant and entertain the customers by singing his favorite Johnny Cash tunes. Due to his popularity at selling items at sporting events, Anthony had a personalized belt buckle made for him that was inscribed "King of the Hawkers." Several weeks later, Ding Ding's picture appeared in the local newspaper, *The Times-Picayune*, showing him proudly wearing his belt buckle.

# Emeril Lagasse

## Bam!

World-renowned chef Emeril Lagasse is the host of "Emeril Live" and "The Essence of Emeril" on the Food Network. His restaurants include Emeril's, Delmonico's, and NOLA in New Orleans; Emeril's, The New Orleans Fish House, and Delmonico Steakhouse in Las Vegas; and Emeril's in the cities of Atlanta, Orlando, and Miami. He also produces a line of cookware, spices, and sauces, and has had several cookbooks published.

Emeril has been a regular customer at Uglesich's since his days as the chef of Commander's Palace. His genuine and warm personality has endured a long lasting friendship with Anthony and Gail, who are frequent customers at his restaurants. In 1993, Emeril's first cookbook was published entitled *Emeril New Orleans Cooking*. Anthony and Gail received a personal copy that was inscribed, "How can I begin to thank you, with friendship and respect forever, always Emeril". The cookbook featured pictures of the front of Uglesich's restaurant, Emeril and Anthony sitting at one of the tables inside the restaurant, and a picture of Gail and Emily behind the counter taking orders.

In 2002, Emeril Lagasse hosted a special entitled the "Big Easy Bash" that focused on his favorite spots in New Orleans. The show first aired during the week of the Super Bowl on the Food Network, and has been repeated on several occasions. Standing in front of the restaurant, Emeril proclaimed that Uglesich's is one of the best-kept secrets, and the place he thinks of for good Creole food. Upon entering, Emeril was greeted by Anthony, and said he was "craving" the Shrimp and Sausage Patties. Anthony delivered Emeril's order, as well as an extra serving of the Pan-Fried Trout with Grilled Shrimp and the Fried Green Tomatoes topped with remoulade sauce. Anthony encouraged Emeril to sample everything and experience the different tastes and flavors of each dish.

Later, Anthony was interviewed outside the restaurant, and labeled Uglesich's as a mom and pop operation. He marveled at how much the menu had continually changed for the better. The segment ended with Emeril leaving the restaurant with a smile, announcing that it "does not get any better than this."

# Martha Stewart

## Entrepreneur

Martha Stewart is the founder of Martha Stewart Enterprises, which includes her television shows, magazines, and a signature line of home essentials. Upon one of her visits to New Orleans, Martha discovered Uglesich's and would routinely dine at the restaurant when in town. Having tried and liked a variety of the specialty dishes over the years, Martha sent her staff to New Orleans to interview Anthony and Gail for a television show that aired in 2001.

The nationally syndicated "Martha Stewart Living Weekday" was dedicated to Martha's favorite places in New Orleans. The show opened with a visit to Cafe du Monde, and later Martha went boating and shucked oysters with P & J Oysters. The last segment of the show began with Martha receiving a brief history of Uglesich's from Anthony and Gail.

Anthony and Martha proceeded to the kitchen, where upon Anthony demonstrated the steps of preparing an Oyster Po-Boy sandwich. Martha helped dress the topside of the French bread and placed the large fried oysters on the bottom side of the loaf. Upon taking her first bite, Martha declared she believed it was the best po-boy in New Orleans.

The next segment featured Gail, with the assistance of Martha, preparing Oysters Shooters. First, the oysters were sautéed on the stove, with the sauce being prepared from scratch to cover the oysters. Martha sampled the oysters and loved the sauce, but her personal favorite sauce is the remoulade that is used over the Fried Green Tomatoes. The show ended with the Tip of the Day, in which

Anthony prepared fried outlaw (small) catfish, which is skinless and boneless. Martha commented that all the fried items were light and not greasy.

The show has aired several times, and customers from all over the United States have informed Anthony and Gail of having seen them on the show.

# Ti Martin

## The Brennans

Ti Martin is the daughter of Ella Brennan, whose family has been in the restaurant business for over fifty years. She is a cookbook author, and along with her cousin Lally manages Commander's Palace. In August 2002, Ti hosted her favorite places in New Orleans on the show "My Country, My Kitchen" that aired on the Food Network. The show opens with Ti giving a history and tour of Commander's Palace.

Later the viewers are introduced to Marcel Bienvue, who used to work at Commander's Palace for a short time. Marcel has co-authored several books with Emeril Lagasse and is the food editor for *The "Times-Picayune,* her articles appearing each Thursday in the "Food Section. Ti mentions how much she has learned from Marcel, who is extremely well respected. The two ladies then went through the process of purchasing and preparing the ingredients for jambalaya.

The second to last segment features Ti proclaiming Uglesich's as the best spot for an oyster po-boy. She compared a po-boy to a submarine sandwich, noting that a po-boy has crispy French bread. If she could have one last meal, she says, it would have to be a dressed oyster po-boy. According to Ti, Uglesich's knows the art of frying without their fried products being fatty. She explained that when you hear the crackling sound from the fryer, the steam is released and grease is not going into the product. As Lally and Ti took their first bites, Ti exclaimed that it was the best po-boy she has ever eaten.

*Anthony Uglesich and Paul Varisco at the Party*

# The First Private Party

## Hosted by Mica and Ahmet Ertegun

Ahmet Ertegun, the co-chairman and co-chief executive officer of Atlantic records, is a frequent visitor to New Orleans. On one of his visits, he contacted a local friend, Karen Wood, about having lunch with him and some of his guests. Karen remembered her friend Paul Varisco had taken her to eat at Uglesich's and contacted Paul about joining them at the restaurant for lunch. The meal left a lasting impression on Ahmet, who contacted Paul several months later to inquire about the restaurant's hosting a private party. Ahmet, his wife Mica, and Paul sampled several dishes at the restaurant. Afterward, the three met with Anthony and Gail and plans were finalized for Uglesich's to host its first private party in May 1989.

The party was in honor of Sid Bass, one of the billionaire Bass brothers of Fort Worth, Texas, and his bride, the former Mercedes Kellogg. The party started around 8:30 P.M. with all the guests arriving by limousines. Some of the more notable names in attendance that night included Oscar de la Renta, Mary McFadden, Barbara Howard, the Albert Taubmans, Albert Finney, and one of the Kissingers. Outside the building two security guards were posted to patrol the area, while inside all tables were covered with white tablecloths, white napkins, and small-lighted candles to provide an intimate but fun setting. In the corner of the restaurant, saxophone player Larry James Hamilton provided entertainment by performing many hits such as "Amen," "When the Saints Go Marching In," and "Mustang Sally." The planned menu started with Crawfish Bisque, followed by Lump Crab Meat Salad, and Marinated Crab Fingers. The main course included Fried Oysters and Shrimp, Barbecued Shrimp, Soft Shell Crabs, Crawfish Hugo, and Grilled Shrimp. At the request of Mica, the guests were served Bolla Soave, a light white Italian wine, with their meal, and later coffee. After dinner, the guests continued to listen to music, with some displaying their enjoyment by dancing on top of the wooden chairs.

The party ended after midnight, with a complete story of the event featured in the "Living" section of *The Times-Picayune*. Gail marveled at meeting such famous people and described the night as "a dream come true" for the restaurant to host such a special party.

*Plate setting at the Party*

*Tables at the Party*

*More tables at the Party*

# The Building

## A Landmark since the 1880s

The sturdy wood building, sitting atop a cement chain wall, was built in the 1800s and has withstood several hurricanes and major street flooding. In 1995, the first major renovations occurred when the old rotten wood was replaced with new treated lumber. The building was sanded and painted a tan color trimmed in light blue. Neal Witmer and Stephen Hassinger performed all of the work, and the renovations received a major story in *The Times-Picayune.* Customers had to be reassured that the restaurant would retain its charm and atmosphere.

The interior of the building still has the same concrete walls and floor as when the building first opened in 1927. Over the years, new and updated equipment have been added in the kitchen and the front counter. A new hood and better ventilation system were installed. As a result, customers no longer had a distinctive smell of where they had lunch. The open kitchen remains a fixture, because Anthony likes it that way, and he says "It's easy for us to go in and out, and if a customer wants to go back there, they can." A new ceiling was installed, and today paintings from local artists hang on the walls.

*Outside view of Uglesich's*

# Word of Mouth
## Travel Guides and National Publications

While the restaurant has never advertised, the following travel guides and national magazines have helped spread the word around the country of the unique flavors of the restaurant. The following are published comments about Uglesich's, as well as specific recommendations:

*The Complete Idiot's Travel Guide to New Orleans* lists Uglesich's as an inexpensive lunch-only restaurant, but notes that one should be prepared for long lines. "It's dangerous to call any one place 'the best in New Orleans,' but it's mighty tempting to make an exception for this tiny, crowded place that serves some of the most divine seafood dishes in town."

*Frommer's* "swears" that the restaurant is worth the wait to be seated, and notes that the best chefs in town have lunch at Uglesich's.

*Avant Guide, New Orleans* recommends the Barbecue Shrimp, Oysters, Shrimp Creole, Crawfish Etoufee, and Angry Shrimp as some of their favorites. "Go directly to Uglesich's, do not pass Go. In other words, don't miss this spot, even if you have to wait for one of the few seats to become available."

*Zagat Survey, New Orleans Restaurants* praises Uglesich's menu as "the greatest seafood around with the freshest and best oysters around and other superb eats that keep it jammed, so go early, and go hungry."

*Rolling Stone Magazine* listed Uglesich's as having the best po-boy sandwich.

*Boston Sunday Globe* suggested trying Uglesich's for a "genuine New Orleans lunch."

*The New York Times* mentioned that when former Atlanta mayor Andrew Young travels to New Orleans, his favorite lunch spot is Uglesich's, with his favorite dish being the large Oyster Po-boy sandwich.

*Gourmet Magazine* listed Uglesich's as one of the twenty best restaurants in New Orleans, and "tops for fun".

*Conde Nast Traveler* rated Uglesich's as one of the best places to eat in the United States. The magazine recommended the Soft Shell Crab and Shrimp Uggie.

*Fortune Magazine* listed Uglesich's as one of the top restaurants in New Orleans and the United States for Fried Soft Shell Crabs

*Southern Magazine* was extremely impressed with the Fried Green Tomatoes with remoulade sauce: "You'll want to tell your mother about those. It's your savory secret."

Chapter Five

# New Recipes

When the restaurant is closed for three months during the summer, Anthony and Gail are busy in their kitchen experimenting and developing new recipes. The following are some of the newest creations served at Uglesich's.

# Cheese Delight

## Shrimp with Melted Cheese

1 tbsp. of butter or margarine
1 small onion, coarsely chopped
1 jalapeno, remove seeds and chop coarsely
1 tomato, diced
1 cup of whipping cream
1 cup of shredded sharp cheddar cheese
$\frac{1}{2}$ cup or 2 slices of Velveeta cheese, broken
    into small pieces
$\frac{1}{2}$ lb. of small shrimp, peeled and deveined
$\frac{1}{2}$ tsp. of salt
$\frac{1}{8}$ tsp. of black pepper
1 pinch of cayenne
Day-old French bread, thinly sliced

Melt the butter or margarine in a saucepan and set on medium heat.

Sauté the onions, jalapeno, and tomatoes until translucent.

Add the whipping cream and cook for 2 to 3 minutes.

Slowly add the cheddar and Velveeta cheese until completely melted.

Fold in the shrimp; add the salt, black pepper, and cayenne.

Cook until the shrimp turn pink, which should take only 2 or 3 minutes.

Take off the fire and let sit.

Toast the French bread until crisp or brown.

Place the shrimp and sauce on top of bread.

## Notes

*If you desire to have the sauce spicy, leave the seeds with the jalapenos.*

*The dish must be served warm.*

# Shrimp and Sausage Festival

This recipe is a light, pleasing appetizer.

1 tbsp. of olive oil
2 cloves of garlic, finely chopped
4 shallots, thinly sliced
1 lb. of Chorizo Sausage; remove from casing and coarsely cut into small pieces
2 Roma tomatoes, diced
1 cup of Pinot Grigio Wine
2 cups of clam juice
1 lb. of shrimp, peeled and deveined, leave tails on
1 tsp. of salt
¼ tsp. of black pepper
⅛ tsp. of cayenne
1 pinch of saffron
2 tbsp. of butter, cut into small pieces
1 tsp. of fresh thyme, finely chopped
1 tsp. of fresh basil, finely chopped
1 tsp. of fresh parsley, finely chopped

In a large sauté pan, pour the olive oil and set on medium heat.

When skillet is hot, add garlic, shallots, and Chorizo Sausage and cook for approx. 1 minute.

Add roman tomatoes and cook for 30 seconds.

Add wine, bring to boil, reduce the liquid by half, and lower heat to medium.

Add the clam juice, shrimp, salt, black pepper, cayenne, and saffron.

Cook until shrimp turn pink, then turn off fire.

Add butter, thyme, basil, and parsley.

Stir; once the butter melts, take off stove and let flavors blend in.

# Spaghetti and Shrimp
## With Carbonara Sauce

1 lb. of angel hair pasta
3 tbsp. of extra virgin olive oil
4 cloves of garlic, smashed
¼ lb. of Panchetta, chopped
4 large jumbo eggs
½ cup of whipping cream
½ cup of Imported Pecorino Romano Cheese
1 tsp. of black pepper
1 lb. of large shrimp, peeled, deveined, and
   headless
2 tsp. of salt
⅛ tsp. of cayenne
2 tbsp. of parsley, finely chopped
2 tbsp. of Imported Reggiano Parmesan
   Cheese (optional)

Cook the spaghetti as per directions on the package.

In a large skillet, pour the olive oil and set on medium heat.

When hot, add the garlic and cook until light brown, then discard the garlic from the skillet.

Add the Panchetta and cook until crispy.

While the Panchetta is cooking, prepare the sauce.

Break the eggs in a bowl and whisk.

Add the whipping cream, Romano cheese, and black pepper and stir.

Keep the sauce in the bowl.

When the Panchetta is cooked, add the shrimp and cook until they turn pink.

Drain the cooked pasta and place in the skillet.

Pour the sauce from the bowl and constantly stir for $1^1/_2$ to 2 minutes.

Add the salt and cayenne, sprinkle with parsley, and stir.

Sprinkle the Parmesan cheese on top if desired.

Mix well together to blend in the flavors.

# Hot Dill Pickles

These pickles are prepared for Anthony and the rest of the employees as a snack during the workday.

Canola oil
Dill pickles
Egg Beater
Plain breadcrumbs
Salt
Black pepper
Crystal Hot Sauce

Pour the canola oil into a frying pot and heat at 350 to 360 degrees.

Drain the pickles into a colander.

Pour the Egg Beater into a bowl.

Dip the pickles in the Egg Beater.

Pour the breadcrumbs on a wax paper, and individually dip each pickle lightly with the breadcrumbs.

Place the pickles in the fryer; when they rise to the top, turn pickles over once, take out, and place on a paper towel.

Lightly season with salt and black pepper.

Sprinkle the hot sauce on top.

# Killer
## Butternut Squash and Shrimp Soup

The recipe is a "Killer" due to the amount of time and preparation required. The end result is one of pure joy. Prepare the shrimp stock first.

## Shrimp stock
2 lb. of fresh shrimp
1 medium onion, chopped
1 carrot, chopped
1 celery stalk, chopped
2 cloves of garlic, chopped
1 herb sack

In sack add the following:

1 bay leaf
¼ tsp. of thyme
¼ tsp. of black pepper corn
2 tbsp. of fresh parsley, chopped

Tie sack with twine.

2 qt. of water

Peel the shrimp, saving the shells and heads, and place all into pot.

Add the onions, carrots, celery stalk, garlic, herb sack, and water.

Bring to a boil, then lower heat to a simmer for approximately 1 hour.

Turn off fire, strain the ingredients, let cool, and refrigerate.

The next day remove any excess fat off top and stir well.

# Butternut

2 lb. of butternut squash
4 tbsp. of butter or margarine, softened
Salt
Black pepper
1 zest of an orange
3 tbsp. of honey
¼ tsp. of cinnamon
1 large yellow onion, chopped
1 lb. of cooked shrimp
½ to 1 cup of shrimp stock
2 tsp. of salt
¼ tsp. of white pepper
¼ tsp. of cayenne
4 cups of heavy cream

Preheat oven to 350 degrees.

Cut squash in half.

Scoop out any seeds and string.

Place 4 halves of the cut squash in a baking pan, skin side down.

Take 2 tablespoons of butter and rub inside the squash.

Sprinkle salt and black pepper on top of butternut squash.

Bake in oven for approximately 1 to 1½ hours, or until tender. Stick a fork in the squash after 1 hour.

Take out of oven, let cool, and scoop out the flesh and place in food processor.

Add the honey, zest of orange, cinnamon, butter into processor and puree.

Place the butternut squash puree into a pot; add the remaining 2 tablespoons of butter or margarine.

Take the cut onions and sauté with a little butter.

Place the onions, shrimp, and shrimp stock in mixture and puree.

Add to the butternut squash puree.

Season with salt, white pepper, and cayenne.

Slowly add the heavy cream, and stir.

Serve in a soup bowl.

# Rice Dressing

This recipe was inspired by reading Tony Chachere's cookbook *Cajun Country Cookbook*. Gail and Anthony decided to change some of the ingredients.

½ lb. of lean ground beef
½ lb. of ground pork
1 bunch of scallions, chopped
1 small white onion, chopped
2 stalks of tender celery, chopped
½ small bell pepper, chopped
½ bunch of parsley, chopped
1 cup of raw rice
1 can (10.5 oz.) of cream of mushroom soup
1 can (10.5 oz.) of onion soup
1 tsp. of salt
¼ tsp. of black pepper
⅛ tsp. of cayenne

Preheat oven to 325 degrees.

Mix all ingredients together.

Place in a 2-quart casserole bowl.

Cover tightly with aluminum foil.

Place in oven and bake for 2 hours.

Chapter Six

# Beverages

# MIXED DRINKS

# Bloody Mary

During Jazz Fest, Gail can make up to a hundred Bloody Marys in one day. It is the most popular mixed drink served in the restaurant. Many customers have said this is the best Bloody Mary they have ever tasted.

1 (12 oz.) glass
Ice cubes
¼ tsp. of horseradish
Worcestershire Sauce
Celery salt
Black pepper
⅙ of a piece of lime
3½ oz. of premium vodka
Red Eye Haberno
1 pickled okra

Place ice cubes in the glass.

Add the horseradish.

Drizzle the Worcestershire Sauce over the ice cubes.

Sprinkle the celery salt over the ice.

Sprinkle a little black pepper.

Squeeze the lime in the glass.

Fill the glass half way with premium vodka.

Fill the other half of the glass with Red Eye Haberno.

Stir well and place the pickled okra on top.

# Margarita

## Note

*If you wish to add to salt to rim of the glass, before adding ice take the other squeezed lime and rub on rim. Dip glass in salt and proceed with directions.*

1 (12 oz.) glass
Lime
Ice
Sweetened lime juice
Cointreau
Premium tequila
½ cup of Lem-N-Joy

Cut the lime into six pieces.

Take 2 of the cut limes and squeeze juice into a shaker; do not discard squeezed lime slices.

Fill the glass with ice.

Place one of the squeezed limes into the glass.

Fill the cap from the sweetened lime juice bottle and pour into shaker.

Add two splashes of cointreau into the shaker.

Add three splashes of tequila into the shaker.

Pour the Lem-N-Joy into the shaker.

Shake well.

Pour into glass over ice.

# Whiskey Sour

Ice cubes
¼ cup of dark rum
½ cup of Benchmark bourbon
1 can (6 oz.) of frozen lemonade
1 bottle (10 oz.) of 7-Up

Place the above ingredients in a blender and blend.
Pour into glass.

# Dirty Martini

Ice cubes or crushed ice
3½ oz. of premium vodka or gin
1 tbsp. of olive juice
2 olives

Take the ice and place in shaker.

Pour the vodka or gin in the shaker.

Add the olive juice to the shaker.

Cover the shaker and shake.

Take the cover off, and place the strainer over the liquid part and pour into a martini glass.

Put olives on a toothpick and place in the glass.

# COMPLETE LISTING OF RED
## AND WHITE WINES

## Red Wines

The following is a list of red wines served in the restaurant:

Cotes Du Rhone, Red Phone
Matanza Creek, Merlot
Stonestreet, Cabernet Sauvignon
Penfolds Rawson's Retreat, Merlot
Penfolds "Bin 389," Cabernet Shiraz
Sterling, Merlot
Gundlach Bundschu, Cabernet Sauvignon
La Crema, Pinot Noir
Ravenswood, California Zinfandel

# White Wines

The following is a list of white wines served in the restaurant:

Trimbach, Pinot Blanc
Frattina, Pinot Grigio
Joseph Drouhin Chablis
Ferravi Carano Fume Blanc
Chateau De L'Hyverniere, Muscadet
Veramonte, Sauvignon Blanc
Kendall Jackson, Chardonnay
Simi, Chardonnay
Sonoma Cutrer, Chardonnay
Penfolds Koonunga Hill, Chardonnay
Conundrum
Woodbridge, White Zinfandel
Valadige, Pinot Grigio

# Beer

The following is a listed of imported and exported beers served in the restaurant:

Abita Amber
Turbo Dog
Budweiser
Miller Lite
Coors Lite
Amstel Lite
Corona
Guinness
Buckler, Non Alcoholic
Heineken
Becks
Pilsner Urquell
Red Stripe
Newcastle
Anchor Steam
Sierra Nevada, Pale Ale
Peroni
Chimay, Grand Reserve

# Glossary

# Terms

*Sauté*

Frying slowly with a small amount of oil or butter in a pan. Frequent stirring is important to distribute the flavors and prevent scorching.

*Egg Beater*

An egg substitute that can be purchased in any local grocery store.

*Translucent*

To shine through, or until the vegetables turn soft.

*Scallions*

Green onions.

*Devein*

To remove the vein or black strip from the back of shrimp.

*Pestle*

A tool used to pound the ingredients into a mortar.

*Parboil*

To partly cook a vegetable, or not boil thoroughly.

*Julienne*

To cut fruit or vegetables into thin strips.


*Ladle*

A long handle with a spoon at the end used to pour the sauce.


*Butterflied*

When the back of a shrimp is cut and spread open.


*Stock pot*

A special pot that is use to prepare soups.


*Tongs*

A device having two arms that is used to pick up objects.

# Index